HAWAII TRIVIA

HAWAII TRIVIA

COMPILED BY ED. CASSIDY

Rutledge Hill Press
Nashville, Tennessee

Published in Nashville, Tennessee, by Rutledge Hill Press,
211 Seventh Avenue North, Nashville, Tennessee 37219. Distrib-
uted in Canada by H.B. Fenn & Company, Ltd., 34 Nixon Road,
Bolton, Ontario L7E 1W2.

Typography by D&T/Bailey Typesetting, Inc., Nashville, Tennessee.

Library of Congress Cataloging-in-Publication Data
Cassidy, Ed., 1954–
    Hawaii trivia / compiled by Ed. Cassdy
      p. cm.
    ISBN 1-55853-422-9 (pbk.)
     1. Hawaii—Miscellanea. I. Title.
DU623.C34   1996
996.9—dc20   96-30474
                         CIP

Printed in the United States of America.
1 2 3 4 5 6 7 8 9 — 99 98 97 96

PREFACE

There are countless answers to the question "what distinguishes Hawaii as the most unique place on earth?" The natural beauty of the islands is unmatched. Its history is a delicate balance between the grand and the tragic, and its culture is a colorful mix of local personalities with worldwide influences.

So this book is designed to entertain, enlighten, and even test a kamaaina's knowledge with questions and answers about their island paradise. And whether visiting Hawaii for the first or fifteenth time, the following pages will take malihinis on an island by island and topic by topic tour of Hawaiian discoveries.

Above all, *Hawaii Trivia* is a compilation of facts, frivolities, and fables that celebrate the one obvious answer we've known all along: "Hawaii no ka oi."

Ed. Cassidy

CONTENTS

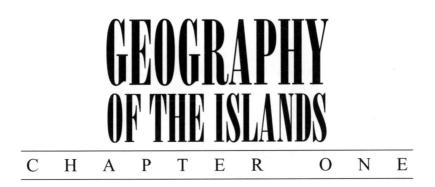

GEOGRAPHY OF THE ISLANDS

CHAPTER ONE

AROUND OAHU

Q. What is Oahu's nickname?

A. The Gathering Place.

Q. How many square miles make up Oahu?

A. 608. It is the third largest of the Hawaiian Islands.

Q. What is the highest peak on the island?

A. Mount Kaala, rising 4,020 feet above sea level.

Q. What is Oahu's offficial flower?

A. The ilima.

Q. What is the official color of Oahu?

A. Golden orange.

Q. What percent of Hawaii's population lives on Oahu?

A. More than 75 percent.

Q. What percent of Hawaii's hotel rooms are found on Oahu?

A. 90 percent.

Q. What does *Honolulu* mean?

A. Sheltered bay.

Q. Who gave Honolulu Harbor its original name of Fair Haven in 1793?

A. William Brown, captain of the English frigate *Butterworth*.

Q. The reef runway at Honolulu International Airport was designed for what emergency?

A. An alternate landing site for space shuttles.

Q. What does every visitor receive at the Hilo Hattie Fashion Factory?

A. A free shell lei.

Q. How many aloha wear garments are produced every month at the Hilo Hattie Fashion Factory?

A. More than fifty thousand.

Q. Who was ordained in 1864 in the Cathedral of Our Lady of Peace?

A. Father Damien.

Q. How many tropical plant species are cultivated in Foster Botanical Gardens?

A. More than four thousand.

———◆———

Q. What school used to be located in the herb garden at the Foster Botanical Garden ?

A. Hawaii's first Japanese language school.

———◆———

Q. What happened to the school in 1941?

A. An errant artillery shell exploded in a room of students during the bombing of Pearl Harbor.

———◆———

Q. How much can coconuts from Foster Botanical Garden's double-coconut palm weigh?

A. As much as fifty pounds.

———◆———

Q. Besides being buried in a pink granite tomb in Oahu Cemetery, what is Alexander Cartwright best known for?

A. Inventing the game of baseball.

———◆———

Q. Plans were announced to tear down Queen Emma's Summer Palace in 1913 and build what?

A. A baseball field.

———◆———

Q. What group intervened and saved the Summer Palace from being torn down?

A. The Daughters of Hawaii Preservation Society. The society still manages the museum today.

———◆———

Q. What is Pensacola Street's namesake?

A. The battleship on which King Lunalilo traveled from Honolulu to Hilo in 1873.

Q. What is Punchbowl, besides the site of the National Memorial Cemetery of the Pacific?

A. An extinct volcanic crater.

◆

Q. How many names of servicemen missing in action are listed on the Courts of the Missing monument in the National Memorial Cemetery of the Pacific?

A. 28,783.

◆

Q. What is the name of the thirty-foot statue towering above the Courts of the Missing?

A. *Columbia.* The statue represents a mother's anguish for her lost children.

◆

Q. Why did ancient Hawaiians call Punchbowl "the hill of human sacrifice"?

A. Human sacrifices were performed there to appease the gods.

◆

Q. How many soldiers are buried in Punchbowl?

A. More than twenty-five thousand.

◆

Q. How many people were left homeless by the 1886 Chinatown fire, which started in a restaurant at Smith and Hotel Streets?

A. More than seven thousand.

◆

Q. Why was Chinatown intentionally burned in 1900?

A. To stop the spread of bubonic plague. Only three buildings were planned to be burned by the Department of Health, but strong winds helped fan a fire that destroyed forty acres of homes and businesses.

◆

Q. How many people were left homeless by the 1900 Chinatown fire?

A. More than four thousand.

Q. Why is there a statue in Chinatown of Sun Yat Sen, founder of the Republic of China in 1911?

A. Dr. Sun lived and studied in Hawaii during his youth.

———◆———

Q. Who gave the statue as a gift to Honolulu in 1976?

A. The government of Taiwan.

———◆———

Q. Who was Jose Rizal, immortalized in a statue in Chinatown?

A. The Philippine revolutionary leader who was executed in 1896. The statue was erected by the Filipina Society of Hawaii.

———◆———

Q. Chinatown sidewalks along Nuuanu Avenue are made of what?

A. The discarded stone ballasts of trade ships from the 1800s.

———◆———

Q. The Izumo Taisha Shinto Shrine, confiscated by the city during World War II, was returned to its congregation in what year?

A. 1962.

———◆———

Q. Why did Kamehameha the Great move his royal residence from Waikiki to the edge of Honolulu Harbor in 1809?

A. So he could monitor ships trading with Hawaii.

———◆———

Q. What did Kamehameha the Great have stored in warehouses along Honolulu Harbor?

A. Weapons that had been traded for Hawaii's sandalwood.

———◆———

Q. Where was Honolulu's business district centered for more than a century?

A. Along five blocks of Merchant Street.

Q. Where was Hawaii's first electric elevator?

A. In the Stangenwald Building on Merchant Street. Built in 1901 and towering six stories above the street, it was one of Hawaii's tallest buildings at the time.

◆

Q. Why was the Yokohama Specie Bank Building at Merchant and Bethel Streets considered the first fireproof structure built in Hawaii?

A. Its window and door frames were lined with copper.

◆

Q. What is now headquartered in the Yokohama Specie Bank Building?

A. *Honolulu Magazine*, the oldest continuously published periodical west of the Mississippi.

◆

Q. Who founded what is now known as *Honolulu Magazine* as *Paradise of the Pacific* in 1888?

A. King David Kalakaua.

◆

Q. What was the original name of Murphy's Bar and Grill on Merchant Street?

A. The Royal Saloon. It opened in 1890 and was a favorite hangout of King Kalakaua.

◆

Q. What is carved into the pillars of the Alexander & Baldwin Building, built in 1929?

A. The Chinese symbols for prosperity and long life.

◆

Q. What made the Aloha Tower so unique when it opened in 1921?

A. It was the tallest building in Hawaii, standing ten stories high.

◆

Q. What once stood on the site now occupied by the Hawaii Maritime Center and Museum at Pier Seven?

A. King Kalakaua's boathouse.

Q. How old is the *Falls of Clyde*, the vessel docked at Pier Seven?

A. The four-masted ship was built in Glasgow, Scotland, in 1878.

———◆———

Q. For what purpose was the *Falls of Clyde* used before it became an oil tanker?

A. The ship was used to carry sugar and passengers between Hilo and San Francisco.

———◆———

Q. What was planned for the *Falls of Clyde* before the Bishop Museum bought it in 1963?

A. It was to be sunk off Vancouver, British Columbia, to help create a breakwater.

———◆———

Q. What is significant about the *Hokulea*, the double-hull canoe that is frequently docked at Pier Seven?

A. The sixty-foot canoe is a replica of the type of vessel that first brought Polynesians to Hawaii. Using only ancient navigational equipment and charts, the *Hokulea* continues to be used in retracing the sailing routes of ancient Hawaiians to Tahiti and throughout the Pacific.

———◆———

Q. Why is the 1883 *Kamehameha the Great* statue only a copy of the original?

A. The original was lost at sea off the coast of the Falkland Islands on its way to Hawaii.

———◆———

Q. What happened to the original *Kamehameha the Great* statue?

A. Years after it was lost, it was discovered in a Port Stanley junk shop by an American sea captain. It was sold to King Kalakaua, who had it placed in front of the courthouse in Kapaau, near the Big Island birthplace of Kamehameha the Great.

———◆———

Q. Who designed the *Kamehameha the Great* statue?

A. Thomas R. Gould.

Q. How much did King Kalakaua pay him for the statue?

A. Ten thousand dollars.

◆

Q. Where is a second copy of the *Kamehameha the Great* statue located?

A. In Statuary Hall of the Capitol in Washington, D.C. This copy was made from molds of the Honolulu statue.

◆

Q. Since federal law allows each state two statues of great personages in Statuary Hall, who also represents Hawaii in Washington, D.C.?

A. Father Damien.

◆

Q. Who modeled for the *Kamehameha the Great* statue?

A. John Baker, a businessman and friend of King Kalakaua.

◆

Q. Why did King Kalakaua select a half-Caucasian, half-Hawaiian local resident to model for the *Kamehameha the Great* statue?

A. He believed the statue would be more visually appealing to foreigners.

◆

Q. What is placed on the *Kamehameha the Great* statue every June 11, a state holiday honoring the king?

A. Flower leis. Some of these leis measure up to twelve feet long.

◆

Q. Until the new state capitol was built in 1969, where did Hawaii's Senate and House of Representatives meet?

A. In Iolani Palace. The Senate met in the dining room, and the House of Representatives met in the throne room.

◆

Q. The governor's eleven-thousand-dollar desk is made of what material?

A. Koa wood.

Q. Who designed the intricate mosaic on the floor of the state capitol?

A. Tadashi Sato.

———◆———

Q. What did Bumpei Akaji design across from the state capitol?

A. A nine-foot copper-and-brass sculpture that holds an eternal flame honoring Hawaii's men and women who died in World War II.

———◆———

Q. What three things does the statue of Queen Liliuokalani, located between the state capitol and Iolani Palace, clutch in its hands?

A. A copy of Kumulipu, a cherished chant detailing Hawaii's creation; the proposed 1893 constitution, which would have restored full power to the monarchy; and the music for "Aloha Oe," written by the queen.

———◆———

Q. How did Beretania Street get its name?

A. It was adapted from native Hawaiians attempting to pronounce "Brittania."

———◆———

Q. What Honolulu structure had running water before the Capitol Building in Washington, D.C., and electricity before the White House and Buckingham Palace?

A. Iolani Palace, completed in 1882. The structure has the distinction of being the only royal palace on American soil.

———◆———

Q. Between what two locations was Hawaii's first telephone line link connected?

A. Iolani Palace and King Kalakaua's boathouse.

———◆———

Q. What are the gems found in each crown of King Kalakaua and Queen Kapiolani, on display at Iolani Palace?

A. Five hundred twenty-one diamonds, fifty-four pearls, twenty opals, eight rubies, eight emeralds, one garnet, and six polished kukui nuts.

Q. When were the jewels in King Kalakaua's crown stolen?

A. Shortly after the overthrow of the monarchy in 1893.

◆

Q. Who stole the jewels?

A. George Ryan. Ryan was an American soldier serving under the provisional government assigned to guard Iolani Palace.

◆

Q. In what year was King Kalakaua's vandalized crown restored?

A. 1925. Funds were appropriated by the territorial legislature to finance the crown's restoration.

◆

Q. How are the polished Douglas fir floors of Iolani Palace protected?

A. Visitors are required to wear cloth booties over their shoes.

◆

Q. Who crowned King Kalakaua in 1883 in the coronation bandstand on the grounds of Iolani Palace?

A. Kalakaua crowned himself and then crowned his queen, Kapiolani.

◆

Q. What was formerly on the grassy mound, which is now surrounded by a wrought iron fence, near Iolani Palace?

A. The tomb of Kamehameha II and Queen Kamamalu. The tombs were moved in 1865 to the Royal Mausoleum.

◆

Q. Since what year has Washington Place, the former home of Queen Liliuokalani, served as the governor's residence?

A. 1921.

◆

Q. What was the first official government structure to be built in Hawaii?

A. Aliiolani Hale (House of Heavenly Kings).

Q. What has been housed in Aliiolani Hale since it opened in 1874?

A. The Hawaii Supreme Court.

———◆———

Q. Aliiolani Hale was originally built as what?

A. The royal palace.

———◆———

Q. What did Sanford Dole declare from the steps of Aliiolani Hale in 1893?

A. The overthrow of the Hawaiian monarchy.

———◆———

Q. How many coral blocks were used in the construction of Kawaiahao Church?

A. Fourteen thousand. Each block was individually cut from ocean reefs.

———◆———

Q. How much do many of the coral blocks weigh?

A. One thousand pounds each.

———◆———

Q. During what years was Kawaiahao Church constructed?

A. 1838 through 1842.

———◆———

Q. Who donated Kawaiaho Church's clock?

A. Kamehameha III in 1850. The clock was built in Boston.

———◆———

Q. Who said "Ua mau ke ea o ka aina i ka pono" (The life of the land is perpetuated in righteousness) in a speech at Kawaihao Church in 1843?

A. Kamehameha III. It remains the official motto of the state of Hawaii.

Q. Where was the Mission Houses Museum's Frame House originally built before it was dismantled, shipped to Hawaii, and reassembled in 1821?

A. Massachusetts.

Q. In what year was Honolulu Hale (City Hall) built?

A. 1929.

Q. Who supervised the start of construction of St. Andrew's Cathedral in 1867?

A. Queen Emma, widow of Kamehameha IV.

Q. Who is pictured in the stained glass of St. Andrew's Cathedral?

A. Rev. Thomas Staley, He was Hawaii's first Anglican bishop, sent by Queen Victoria.

Q. What used to stand in Thomas Square?

A. The Honolulu fort.

Q. What important historical event took place in Thomas Square during 1843?

A. British Admiral Richard Thomas returned control of Hawaii to Kamehameha III. Several months earlier, British officers had seized the Honolulu fort by force and declared Hawaii a part of the British Empire—an action not approved by Britain's Queen Victoria.

Q. How old are the Egyptian facades surrounding the Spanish Court inside Honolulu Academy of Arts?

A. They date back to 2500 B.C.

Q. The 1925 estate that is now home of the Contemporary Museum once belonged to whom?

A. Mrs. Charles Montague Cooke.

Q. What does Mrs. Cooke's other former home now house?

A. The Honolulu Academy of Arts.

———◆———

Q. Who owns the Honolulu lingerie store Brief Essentials?

A. Susan Midler, Bette Midler's younger sister.

———◆———

Q. What is Magic Island?

A. A forty-three-acre man-made peninsula jutting out from Ala Moana Beach Park.

———◆———

Q. What does *Ala Moana* mean?

A. Pathway to the sea.

———◆———

Q. When it opened in 1959, how was Ala Moana Shopping Center billed?

A. As the world's largest shopping center, with 150 stores. It still ranks as one of the world's largest open-air shopping centers.

———◆———

Q. Who donated the land for Punahou School, Hawaii's most famous private school, founded in 1841?

A. Queen Kaahumanu, Kamehameha's favorite wife. It was founded in 1841 for the education of the Congregationalist missionaries' children.

———◆———

Q. How many full-time students enrolled in the University of Hawaii when it opened in 1908?

A. Five, with twelve teachers.

———◆———

Q. What was first planted in Manoa Valley in the early 1800s?

A. Coffee. The trees were eventually shipped to the Big Island town of Kona.

Q. What is the name of Oahu's bus system?

A. TheBus.

Q. What happened to Robert Louis Stevenson's Waikiki grass hut?

A. It was dismantled and moved to the grounds of the Waioli Tea Room in 1926.

Q. How many acres make up Waikiki?

A. 507, less than a square mile.

Q. On an average day, how many tourists are in Waikiki?

A. About sixty thousand.

Q. How many Oahu residents live in Waikiki?

A. About twenty-five thousand.

Q. Approximately how much do visitors spend in Waikiki every year?

A. $3.9 billion.

Q. How much was spent to improve Waikiki during the years of 1986 through 1988?

A. More than $350 million.

Q. How many establishments catering to tourists were recorded in Waikiki in the early 1990s?

A. 33,000 hotel rooms and more than 450 restaurants, 350 bars, and 1,000 shops.

Q. What is Waikiki's annual hotel occupancy rate?

A. 80 percent.

———◆———

Q. How many miles of beach are located in Waikiki?

A. 1.4.

———◆———

Q. When did beaches in Waikiki noticably begin to erode?

A. Around 1914, when the Army Corps of Engineers destroyed part of the offshore reef to build gun batteries.

———◆———

Q. What is the name of the beach in front of the Hilton Hawaiian Village?

A. Kahanamoku Beach, named for Hawaii's champion surfer and swimmer.

———◆———

Q. Why is the small beach area in front of the Halekulani Hotel named Gray's Beach?

A. A small boarding house named Gray's-by-the-Beach occupied the spot in the 1920s.

———◆———

Q. What is the Kapahulu Groin?

A. A walled storm drain that juts out from Kuhio Beach in Waikiki.

———◆———

Q. Why is San Souci Beach, in front of the New Otani Kaimana Beach Hotel, nicknamed "Dig Me Beach"?

A. Because of the busty beauties and male bodybuilders that frequently sun and strut in microscopic swimsuits.

———◆———

Q. How many hotel rooms make up the Hilton Hawaiian Village?

A. 2,522 rooms.

Q. Who designed the Hilton Hawaiian Village Dome, once "The Home of Don Ho," and the first geodesic dome built in the United States?

A. Buckminster Fuller in 1959.

———◆———

Q. What is suspended over the bar at the Hard Rock Cafe?

A. A 1959 Cadillac "woody" wagon.

———◆———

Q. Where is the U.S. Army Museum of Hawaii located?

A. Inside Battery Randolph, a 1911 coastal artillery battery structure.

———◆———

Q. Why is the King Kalakaua statue at the entrance to Waikiki a 1991 gift from a Japanese American citizens committee?

A. It is a tribute to the Hawaiian king who signed the treaty allowing Japanese laborers to come to Hawaii more than one hundred years ago.

———◆———

Q. How large was the coconut grove that surrounded the Royal Hawaiian Hotel when it first opened?

A. Twenty acres.

———◆———

Q. What did Mr. and Mrs. Nelson Rockefeller, as well as Mr. and Mrs. Henry Ford II, enjoy at the Royal Hawaiian Hotel?

A. Honeymoons.

———◆———

Q. Which famous Paris fashion and design houses have boutiques in Waikiki?

A. Hermes, Chanel, Celine, Christian Dior, and Louis Vuitton.

———◆———

Q. According to popular mythology, what are the large stones on the Diamond Head side of the Moana Hotel?

A. The Wizard Stones. They are believed to be endowed with the healing powers of four Tahitian prophets.

Q. What are the names of the four Tahitian prophets represented by each of the Wizard Stones?

A. Kapaemahu, Kinohi, Kapuni, and Kahaloa.

Q. Who painted the huge murals in First Hawaiian Bank's Waikiki branch depicting the arrivals of various ethnic groups to Hawaii?

A. Artist Jean Charlot.

Q. Who first owned the Waikiki Circle Hotel, which opened in 1962?

A. Emma Kwock Chun, the first Asian woman to own a hotel in Waikiki.

Q. What controversy still surrounds the placement of the statue of Duke Kahanamoku, Hawaii's Olympic and surfing legend?

A. The statue, unveiled in 1990, faces Kalakaua Avenue with its back to the Pacific Ocean. The controversy stems from the fact that all surfers know it is dangerous to stand with your back to the ocean.

Q. How tall is the atrium in the Hyatt Regency Waikiki?

A. Ten stories, with a three-story waterfall.

Q. How large is the aquarium inside the lobby of the Pacific Beach Hotel?

A. The 280,000-gallon aquarium is three stories high.

Q. Where is the Mohandas Gandhi statue located?

A. At the entrance to the Honololo Zoo.

Q. Who gave the statue to the the people of Hawaii in 1990?

A. The Gandhi Memorial International Foundation.

Q. When did the Honolulu Zoo unofficially open?

A. 1914.

———◆———

Q. When did the Honolulu Zoo officially open?

A. 1947, when it occupied its current forty-two-acre site in Kapiolani Park.

———◆———

Q. What is the only marine research site to breed the Palauan nautilus in captivity?

A. Waikiki Aquarium.

———◆———

Q. What is the Waikiki Natatorium?

A. A one-hundred-meter saltwater pool and cement bleachers with enough seating for two thousand. The Natatorium was built in 1927.

———◆———

Q. What group is honored by the Waikiki Natatorium?

A. Hawaiians who served in World War I.

———◆———

Q. What event did the Territory of Hawaii hope to attract by building the Waikiki Natatorium?

A. The Olympics.

———◆———

Q. Who set world swimming records in 1927 in the Waikiki Natatorium?

A. Johnny Weissmuller and Hawaii native Buster Crabbe.

———◆———

Q. How high is the summit of Diamond Head?

A. Seven hundred sixty feet above sea level.

Q. What ruins are found on Diamond Head?

A. A heiau (temple) for human sacrifice.

———◆———

Q. How did Mount Leahi, the volcanic crater extinct for 150,000 years, acquire its nickname of Diamond Head?

A. Sailors in 1825 thought they had discovered diamonds inside the crater. The "diamonds" turned out to be worthless calcite crystals.

———◆———

Q. What now occupies the inside of Diamond Head crater?

A. Federal Aviation Administration and Hawaii National Guard buildings.

———◆———

Q. What is considered the Beverly Hills of Hawaii?

A. The Kahala residential area.

———◆———

Q. When were Koko Crater and Koko Head formed?

A. About ten thousand years ago during Oahu's last volcanic eruptions.

———◆———

Q. In what year was Hanauma Bay established as a marine life conservation district?

A. 1967.

———◆———

Q. What does *hanauma* mean?

A. Curved.

———◆———

Q. How many people visit the one-hundred-acre Hanauma Bay every year?

A. Approximately 2.5 million.

Q. How many people visit the twelve-hundred-mile Great Barrier Reef in Australia every year?

A. Approximately 2.5 million.

———◆———

Q. What is the Toilet Bowl?

A. A circular rock formation on a ledge near Hanauma Bay where waves "flush" in and out of an opening.

———◆———

Q. What tragedy occurs more at Hanauma Bay than at any other beach in Hawaii?

A. Drownings.

———◆———

Q. What three islands can be seen from Halona Blow Hole on clear days?

A. Maui, Molokai, and Lanai.

———◆———

Q. What is Kaikaimalu, born in captivity at Sea Life Park?

A. The first known "wolphin"—a cross between a whale and a dolphin.

———◆———

Q. How long did it take Sea Life Park staff to remove thirty-eight thousand pounds of flesh from the now-displayed skeleton of a thirty-eight-foot sperm whale?

A. More than two years using antique whaling tools.

———◆———

Q. Where is the world's largest lighthouse lens (thirteen feet by nine feet), which was made in France in 1887?

A. Makapuu Lighthouse.

———◆———

Q. What creatures guard the mythical dry lava tube that runs all the way to Molokai and can only by accessed by an underwater cave in Makapuu?

A. Sharks.

Q. How did Manana Island get the nickname of Rabbit Island?

A. A Spanish sea captain let rabbits loose on the island with the approval of Kamehameha the Great.

◆

Q. What two creatures share the same burrows on Rabbit Island?

A. Ferral rabbits and wedge-tailed shearwaters.

◆

Q. What did the residents of Waimanalo do when the Hawaiian monarchy was overthrown?

A. They planned to fight to restore Queen Liliuoklani to the throne, hiding weapons in the sand on Rabbit Island in preparation for an armed revolt. Their plan was discovered before any confrontations took place.

◆

Q. What is Oahu's longest beach?

A. Waimanalo Beach, which is five and a half miles long.

◆

Q. The Old Pali Highway was once nothing more than what?

A. An ancient footpath that was widened and cobblestoned in 1845.

◆

Q. What battle culminated at the Nuuanu Pali Lookout?

A. The 1795 Battle of Nuuanu Valley. The battle was decided when the invading forces of King Kamehameha the Great literally drove the Oahu army over the one-thousand-foot cliffs.

◆

Q. How many skulls have been found at the base of the Nuuanu Pali Lookout cliffs?

A. More than five hundred to date.

◆

Q. Who was buried above ground in a treehouse-style mausoleum in the Valley of the Temples?

A. Exiled Philippine president Ferdinand Marcos. The body remained there until his wife, Imelda, was allowed to return the body to his native country.

Q. Where is the original Byodo-In (Temple of Equality), built in Hawaii in1968 as a replica of the nine-hundred-year-old temple?

A. Uji, Japan.

———◆———

Q. How heavy is the brass bell hanging outside the Byodo-In?

A. Three tons.

———◆———

Q. Who were three of the victims sacrificed in 1794 at the Puu o Mahuka Heiau in Pupukea?

A. Sailors from Captain Vancouver's crew.

———◆———

Q. According to Hawaiian legend, what was Mokolii Island (Chinaman's Hat)?

A. The tail of a vicious dog, cut off by a god and thrown into the sea.

———◆———

Q. In what year did the Church of Jesus Christ of Latter-day Saints complete its Mormon Temple in Laie?

A. 1919. The temple was built on the same land on which they had established their missionary tract in 1864.

———◆———

Q. Where did the pacific army train for jungle warfare during World War II?

A. In the hills above Pupukea Beach.

———◆———

Q. What was the first town to attract tourists?

A. Haleiwa, with an elegant Victorian hotel opening in 1899.

———◆———

Q. Why must all new buildings in Haleiwa be designed to look as if they were built before 1920?

A. To comply with the plantation town's 1984 declaration as a historic, cultural, and scenic district.

Q. What gift did Hawaii's ruling queen give to the Liliuokalani Church, which is still displayed?

A. A wall clock with the twelve letters of the queen's name on the timepiece instead of numbers.

———◆———

Q. Some of the chairs in the Sugar Bar in Waialua Town are made of what?

A. Toilets.

———◆———

Q. What are the stones at Kukaniloko in Wahiawa?

A. Birthing stones dating back to the twelfth century on which chieftesses gave birth to royal heirs.

———◆———

Q. For whom is Schofield Barracks, base of the army's 25th Infantry Division, named?

A. Maj. Gen. John Schofield, who served as superintendent of West Point and commanding general of the U.S. Army.

———◆———

Q. What did Schofield do on his visit to Hawaii in 1873?

A. He pretended to be a tourist while he was actually surveying Pearl River Lagoon (which would later become Pearl Harbor) as a potential U.S. naval port.

———◆———

Q. What beach marks the beginning of Oahu's most extensive coastal wilderness park?

A. Makua Beach.

———◆———

Q. Why was the proposed road connecting Oahu's west shore around Kaena Point never completed?

A. The territorial government attempted in 1954 to use twenty prison inmates to build a road around Kaena Point but was unsuccessful in securing rights-of-way from landowners.

———◆———

Q. What remnants of former transportation routes can still be seen around Kaena Point?

A. Railroad ties and buttresses from Oahu Railway that used to take passengers to Mokuleia until the route was closed in 1947.

Q. What did ancient Hawaiians believe took place at Kaena Point?

A. Souls jumped off the point into death. From death, a god would decide whether the soul was to go to Kahiki (heaven) or a place of eternal night.

Q. What did Maui the demigod attempt to do from Kaena Point?

A. Snare the island of Kauai with a giant coral fishhook and tug it across the sea to join it with Oahu.

Q. What created the Pohaku o Kauai islet off Kaena Point?

A. When Maui fell backward pulling Kauai toward Oahu, a tiny portion broke off and came to rest off Kaena Point.

Q. What is the name of the tree with salmon-colored flowers that grows nowhere else in the world but around Kaena Point?

A. Ohai.

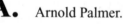

Q. What is the "big golf ball above Yokohama Bay"?

A. The top-secret Kaena Point Missile Tracking station, built in 1958.

Q. Who assisted in the design of Honolulu International Country Club's golf course in the late 1970s?

A. Arnold Palmer.

Q. Who founded the Bishop Museum, opened to the public in 1891 in honor of his wife Bernice Pauahi Bishop (great-granddaughter of Kamehameha the Great)?

A. Charles Reed Bishop, founder of Bishop Bank and a noble in the court of Kamehameha IV.

Q. What hangs from the ceiling of the main hall of the Bishop Museum?

A. The skeleton of a whale.

◆

Q. Kamehameha the Great's cloak, on display in the Bishop Museum, is made of what?

A. More than eighty thousand feathers from native birds, including the now-extinct mamo.

◆

Q. Who designed the USS *Arizona* Memorial in 1962?

A. Alfred Preis. Mr. Preis was a prominent local architect of Austrian descent who had fled from Germany to Hawaii.

◆

Q. What happened to Alfred Preis following the bombing of Pearl Harbor?

A. He was arrested and interned at the Sand Island Detention Center internment camp during the first two years of World War II.

◆

Q. What was Preis careful to do in his design of the memorial?

A. Make sure that no part of the memorial touched or was affixed in any way to the USS *Arizona*.

◆

Q. How many enemy ships did the submarine USS *Bowfin*, now a floating museum, sink during World War II?

A. Forty-four.

◆

Q. How long did it take the USS *Arizona* to sink following a direct hit in the Pearl Harbor bombing on December 7, 1941?

A. Nine minutes.

◆

Q. How many bodies are still entombed in the hull of the USS *Arizona*?

A. 1,102.

Q. What was the average age of enlisted men killed aboard the USS *Arizona*?

A. Nineteen.

AROUND MAUI

Q. What is Maui's nickname?

A. The Valley Isle.

————◆————

Q. How many square miles make up Maui?

A. 729. This figure makes it the second largest Hawaiian island.

————◆————

Q. What are the names of the two volcanoes that formed Maui?

A. Puu Kukui on West Maui and 10,023-foot Haleakala on East Maui.

————◆————

Q. What is the official flower of Maui?

A. The lokelani rose.

————◆————

Q. What is the official color of Maui?

A. Pink.

————◆————

Q. What is the world's largest dormant volcano?

A. Haleakala.

————◆————

Q. What island could fit inside Haleakala Crater?

A. All of Manhattan.

Q. On a clear day, what other islands can be seen from the Puu Ulaula cinder cone atop Haleakala?

A. Molokai, Lanai, Kahoolawe, the Big Island, and Oahu.

◆

Q. When did Haleakala last erupt?

A. 1790.

◆

Q. How deep is the Bottomless Pit, located inside Haleakala Crater along the Halemauu Trail?

A. Sixty-five feet.

◆

Q. What trees were planted in Hosmer Grove in hopes of creating a lumber industry?

A. Douglas fir, Japanese sugi, eucalyptus, and cedar.

◆

Q. Why did a lumber industry never develop?

A. The trees did not grow fast enough due to the high elevation.

◆

Q. Who engineered the extensive roadways around the island?

A. Maui chief Piilani during the fourteenth century.

◆

Q. What entire Maui town was designated a National Historic Landmark in 1962?

A. Lahaina.

◆

Q. What does Lahaina mean?

A. Cruel, merciless sun.

Q. How many banyan trees cover the full acre next to the Pioneer Inn?

A. One.

———◆———

Q. Why was the sprawling banyan tree planted in 1873?

A. To commemorate the fiftieth anniversary of the arrival of the missionaries.

———◆———

Q. The rules "You are not allow in the down stears in the seating room or in the dinering room or in the kitchen when you are drunk," "if you wet or burn you bed you going out," and "only on Sunday you can sleep all day" are still posted for guests at what Maui hotel?

A. The Pioneer Inn, built in 1901.

———◆———

Q. Who built the Pioneer Inn?

A. George Freeland, a member of the Royal Canadian Mounted Police who moved to Lahaina.

———◆———

Q. How many ships would dock in Lahaina Harbor during the 1840s?

A. More than four hundred per year.

———◆———

Q. Why did Queen Keopuolani order the Lahaina fort to be built in 1831?

A. To intidimate and warn unruly sailors and whalers who came ashore from ships docked in Lahaina Harbor.

———◆———

Q. Where did the four remaining cannons at the old Lahaina fort come from?

A. A Russian ship that sank off Honolulu in 1816.

———◆———

Q. How many cannons used to surround the walls of the old Lahaina fort?

A. Forty-seven, most from foreign ships that had been sunk off Hawaiian waters.

Q. The square-rigger *Carthaginian II*, brought to Lahaina Harbor in 1973, was built in what country in 1920?

A. Germany.

Q. What happened to the first *Carthaginian*?

A. It hit a reef and sank in 1972 while being sailed from Lahaina to Honolulu for dry dock repairs.

Q. What ailment did most sailors die of while in Seamen's Hospital during the 1850s and 1860s?

A. "Disreputable disease."

Q. How much of the budget established by Congress for the care of United States seamen worldwide was spent on sick sailors in Hawaii?

A. More than half.

Q. Why did the original Waiola Church, which seated three thousand when it opened in 1832, burn to the ground in 1894?

A. Angry mobs protesting the overthrow of the monarchy torched the church.

Q. Which of the Hawaiian royalty is buried in the Waiola Church cemetery?

A. Queen Keopuolani, the most sacred wife of Kamehameha the Great and the first high-ranking member of royalty to convert to Christianity.

Q. What is the oldest building in Lahaina, built in 1834?

A. The Baldwin House, former home of missionary doctor Rev. Dwight Baldwin.

Q. Why did angry sailors fire cannons in 1827 on the home of missionary William Richards, located next door to the Baldwin House?

A. Richards demanded the Maui governor order the arrest of ships' captains for allowing Hawaiian women to be brought aboard ships.

Q. Angry with both Baldwin and Richards for promoting morality among native women, what did whalers plant in the water ponds around the missionaries' homes?

A. Larvae for Hawaii's first mosquitoes.

Q. What do records show were some of the top crimes that landed sailors in Hale Paahao (Stuck-in-Iron House), Lahaina's prison in the 1850s?

A. Public drunkenness, adultery, working on Sunday, carelessly riding a horse, and fathering illegitimate children.

Q. How could Hawaiians collect rewards from Hale Paahao?

A. By turning in sailors who flirted (and more) with native women.

Q. How much of the Hale Piula royal palace was built during the reign of Kamehameha III?

A. The foundation and steps were all that were ever built.

Q. In 1845, Kamehameha III decided to move Hawaii's capitol from Lahaina to what city?

A. Honolulu.

Q. What were students required to do while attending Lahainaluna School, the first secondary school west of the Rocky Mountains, which opened in 1831?

A. Grow their own food and print their own textbooks.

Q. Who is buried on grounds above the school?

A. David Malo, Hawaiian philosopher, Lahainaluna Seminary graduate, and the first Hawaiian ordained to the Christian ministry.

Q. What did Malo's 1837 writings demand?

A. The establishment of native Hawaiian rights. Malo's writings also contain warnings about the influx of foreigners to the islands.

Q. What was the 1790 Olowalu Massacre in the village south of Lahaina?

A. Simon Metcalfe, captain of the trading ship *Eleanora*, lured more than one hundred Hawaiians out to his ship and then mercilessly shot and killed them.

◆

Q. Why did Metcalfe plot the massacre?

A. To avenge the mysterious death of one of his crewmen.

◆

Q. What was the purpose of the dock built in Kaanapali next to Puu Kekaa (Black Rock)?

A. To facilitate the loading of sugar cane onto boats.

◆

Q. Why was the dock torn down?

A. The Pioneer Mill Company moved its operations to Lahaina Harbor in the early 1900s.

◆

Q. How many tons of natural rock were used in creating the gardens at the Hyatt Regency Maui?

A. Ten thousand tons.

◆

Q. Where is the original of the seventeen-foot-high *Acrobats* sculpture found at the entrance to the Hyatt Regency Maui?

A. In front of the Tower of London.

◆

Q. What sits on the rooftop of the Hyatt Regency Maui?

A. Giant binoculars and a sixteen-inch telescope.

◆

Q. What did it cost to build the Hyatt Regency Maui in 1980?

A. $80 million.

Q. What did Japan's Kokusai Jidosha pay when it bought the hotel seven years later?

A. $319 million.

Q. What is unusual about the Kaanapali Beach Hotel pool?

A. It is shaped like a whale.

Q. What resort was forced to move its location back from the beach when an ancient Hawaiian burial site was discovered as construction began?

A. The Ritz-Carlton Kapalua.

Q. What was formed by Haleakala's last eruption in 1790?

A. Kinau Cape, accessible only by four-wheel drive.

Q. For what person was La Perouse Bay named?

A. The French explorer and first European to set foot on Maui in 1786.

Q. What is Molokini, the tiny islet between Maui and Kahoolawe?

A. The exposed portion of a submerged volcanic crater.

Q. What did the U.S. Navy once use Molokini for?

A. Target practice.

Q. What is the designation for the water surrounding Molokini?

A. A marine conservation district.

Q. What was recently removed from Molokini's crater floor in twenty feet of water?

A. Three live navy bombs.

———◆———

Q. What Maui resort's swimming pool was modeled after one at San Simeon's Hearst Castle in California?

A. The Grand Wailea's one-third-acre pool, which is adjacent to a two-thousand-foot river-like pool.

———◆———

Q. What is the value of the solid gold teapot displayed in Kincha, the Japanese tea house in Wailea?

A. $2 million.

———◆———

Q. What was used to create a reef off of Keawakapu Beach?

A. Bodies of junked cars and old tires filled with concrete.

———◆———

Q. Why is Ulua Beach nicknamed Tarawa Beach?

A. Marines trained on the beach for the invasion of Tarawa.

———◆———

Q. From the mid-1960s to 1972, what stood on Big Beach in Makena?

A. A hippie tent city.

———◆———

Q. On what historical site was the Maui Arts and Culture Center built in 1994?

A. Pa Hula Heiau, a temple dedicated to the traditional Hawaiian dance. Remains of the temple are still visible.

———◆———

Q. Why was Kahului's waterfront burned to the ground in 1900?

A. To curb the spread of bubonic plague.

Q. Duke Kahanamoku's famed six-foot, 150-pound surfboard, on display in the Bailey House, is made of what kind of wood?

A. Redwood.

Q. Why did the missionaries name Kaahumanu Church in honor of the favorite wife of Kamehameha the Great?

A. Kaahumanu often attended services in a grass shack at this site and asked that the permanent church structure be named after her.

Q. Where did Kamehameha finally emerge victorious over Maui's chief Kahekili in 1790?

A. In a bloody battle in Iao Valley.

Q. Who performed the last human sacrifice in 1790 on Maui at Halekii-Pihanakalani Heiau?

A. Kamehameha the Great, following his conquest of Maui, as an offering to the war god Ku.

Q. How wide is the reef off of Waihee Beach—the widest on the island?

A. More than one thousand feet.

Q. Where are more than 90 percent of all carnations used in Hawaii's leis grown?

A. Kula.

Q. Where are most of Hawaii's protea, introduced to the islands in 1965, grown?

A. Kula.

Q. How many varieties of grapes were test grown at Tedeschi Winery at the two-thousand-foot elevation on Haleakala?

A. More than 140 varieties.

Q. What grape was finally chosen to create the Maui wines?

A. The carnelian grape.

———◆———

Q. During what year was the road to Hana built using prison labor?

A. 1927.

———◆———

Q. When was the road to Hana paved?

A. 1962.

———◆———

Q. How long is the road to Hana?

A. Fifty-three miles.

———◆———

Q. How many curves are part of the road to Hana?

A. 617.

———◆———

Q. How many bridges are crossed when traveling the road to Hana?

A. Fifty-four.

———◆———

Q. How many gallons of water are carried every day along the century-old Koolau Ditch irrigation system?

A. 450 million gallons.

———◆———

Q. What did Kamehameha the Great plan to accomplish when he departed from Hana in 1795?

A. Conquer and unite all the islands.

Q. Where was Queen Kaahumanu born in 1768?

A. In a cave on Hana Bay.

Q. Why do clouds always linger over Kauiki Head?

A. It was here that Maui united two lovers for eternity—turning the man into the hill and his lover into the mist above it.

Q. What is Wananalua Church made of?

A. Volcanic rocks taken from the ruins of ancient temples.

Q. What is the only beach in Hawaii made of red volcanic cinder?

A. Hana's Kaihalulu Beach (Red Sand Beach).

Q. What is sacred about the Seven Sacred Pools, also referred to as Oheo Gulch?

A. Nothing. The "sacred" reference was made up by Maui tour guides.

Q. How many pools are found in Oheo Gulch?

A. Twenty-four. They stretch from Waimoku Falls down to the sea.

Q. Who is buried in the tiny Kipahulu Congregational Church cemetery?

A. Charles Lindbergh, who moved to Hana in 1968 and died in 1974.

AROUND MOLOKAI

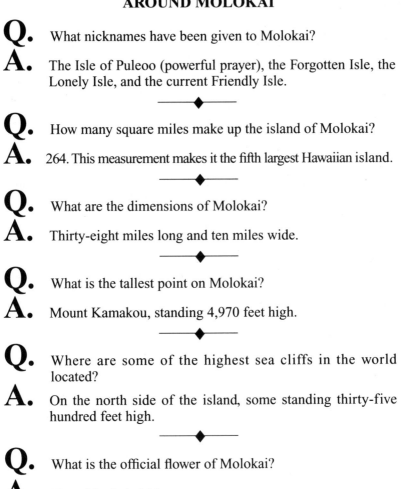

Q. What nicknames have been given to Molokai?

A. The Isle of Puleoo (powerful prayer), the Forgotten Isle, the Lonely Isle, and the current Friendly Isle.

◆

Q. How many square miles make up the island of Molokai?

A. 264. This measurement makes it the fifth largest Hawaiian island.

◆

Q. What are the dimensions of Molokai?

A. Thirty-eight miles long and ten miles wide.

◆

Q. What is the tallest point on Molokai?

A. Mount Kamakou, standing 4,970 feet high.

◆

Q. Where are some of the highest sea cliffs in the world located?

A. On the north side of the island, some standing thirty-five hundred feet high.

◆

Q. What is the official flower of Molokai?

A. The white kukui blossom.

◆

Q. What is the official color of Molokai?

A. Green.

◆

Q. According to the *Molokai News*, what is the population of the island?

A. "6,500 friends."

Q. How did Molokai (barren sea) get its name?

A. Hawaiians thought the island's dry western terrain and inaccessible eastern and northern cliffs seemed inhospitable .

———◆———

Q. Who first conquered Molokai?

A. Oahu chief Peleioholani.

———◆———

Q. What did Peleioholani do when Molokai's kahunas captured and killed the daughter he left behind?

A. He had all of Molokai's chiefs burned alive.

———◆———

Q. Who was the first Caucasian to visit the island in 1786?

A. British Capt. George Dixon. Captain Cook bypassed the island on his voyages.

———◆———

Q. What is the capital of Molokai?

A. Wailuku on Maui. Molokai, as well as Lanai, are part of Maui County.

———◆———

Q. Who is said to have planted Kapuaiwa Grove with more than one thousand coconut palms?

A. Molokai resident Prince Lot, who became Kamehameha V and ruled over Hawaii from 1863 to 1872.

———◆———

Q. What happened to Molokai's honey production, once the largest in the world?

A. An epidemic in the 1930s destroyed the hives.

———◆———

Q. What crops were attempted on Molokai before pineapple?

A. Sugar cane, rice, and cotton.

Q. What is the largest white-sand beach in Hawaii?

A. Papohaku Beach, two miles long and an average three hundred feet wide.

———◆———

Q. What was Papohaku Beach sand used for?

A. To build up Waikiki Beach.

———◆———

Q. What was the original plan for the Kaluakoi resort area in the early 1970s?

A. Four hotels with eleven hundred rooms, twelve hundred condominium units, one thousand homes and a fifteen-acre shopping center.

———◆———

Q. In what year did Kaluakoi Resort, Molokai's first and only luxury hotel with only 240 rooms, open?

A. In 1977.

———◆———

Q. What is the largest man-made, rubber-lined reservoir in the world, holding 1.4 million gallons of water?

A. Kualapuu Reservoir.

———◆———

Q. What were pilings made of in the original Kaunakakai wharf, built in 1898?

A. Coconut trunks.

———◆———

Q. How large is the ancient Keawanui fishpond?

A. It covers fifty-five acres and is enclosed by a two-thousand-foot-long seawall.

———◆———

Q. What did the Hawaii Sugar Planters Association plant at Mapulehu in the 1930s?

A. The world's largest mango grove. The operation eventually failed.

Q. Where were the mango trees imported from?

A. Vietnam, Cambodia, and Laos.

Q. What is the oldest standing church in Hawaii?

A. Kaluaaha Church, built in 1832.

Q. What destroyed the settlement in Halawa Valley?

A. 1946 and 1957 tsunamis.

Q. What is the highest waterfall in Hawaii?

A. Molokai's Kahiwa Falls at 1,750 feet.

Q. How did people with leprosy get to the Kalawao and Kalaupapa settlements on Kalaupapa Peninsula?

A. They were pushed overboard from ships or barges and left to swim to shore or drown.

Q. In what year were those afflicted with leprosy first sent to Kalaupapa?

A. 1866.

Q. In what year did Father Damien arrive in Kalaupapa?

A. 1873.

Q. What did Father Damien do at least once a day?

A. Bury a victim of leprosy.

Q. How many people died of leprosy in Kalaupapa?

A. More than eight thousand.

Q. Of the more than eleven hundred Kalaupapa volunteers who worked with leprosy patients, who was the only one to ever contract the disease?

A. Father Damien.

Q. What churches did Father Damien build on Molokai?

A. St. Joseph's in Kamalo (1874), Our Lady of Sorrows in Kaluaaha (1874), and St. Philomena's in Kalawao (1888).

Q. Why did Father Damien cut holes into the floor of St. Philomena's Church?

A. So that the sick who needed to spit could attend church.

Q. Why is Father Damien now called Blessed Father Damien?

A. He has been beatified by the Vatican and is in the process of canonization.

Q. How large did the leprosy patient population become at Kalaupapa?

A. It peaked at 1,174 in 1890.

Q. How many residents with leprosy now live in Kalaupapa?

A. Fewer than seventy.

Q. What was the first church built in Kalaupapa?

A. Siloama Protestant Church, built in 1866.

Q. What became of babies born in Kalaupapa?

A. After medical care was introduced, newborns were immediately taken from their mothers and sent to Honolulu.

◆

Q. What is peculiar about Kauhako Crater?

A. It extends four hundred feet below sea level and is filled with both fresh and salt water.

◆

Q. Why is the island off of Kaulapapa called Shark Island?

A. Hawaiians believed it was the home of a legendary shark because it resembles the head of a giant shark emerging from the sea.

◆

Q. How large was the fleet of war canoes under the command of Kamehameha the Great when he conquered Molokai at the Pakuhiwa Battlefield?

A. The fleet of canoes stretched for more than four miles.

◆

Q. What is the Smith-Bronte Landing in Kamalo?

A. The site where aviators Ernest Smith and Emory Bronte made an emergency crash landing in 1927 after completing the world's first civilian transpacific flight.

◆

Q. What did Kamehameha the Great do for a full year at Hoolehua?

A. Prepare his army for the invasion of Oahu.

◆

Q. What is unique about Moomomi Beach?

A. It is the only undisturbed coastal sand dune area remaining in Hawaii.

◆

Q. Who founded the Molokai-to-Oahu canoe race in 1952?

A. Albert Edward "Toots" Minvielle.

Q. How long is the race, the first open-ocean canoe race of its kind in the world?

A. It begins at Molokai's Hale O Lono Harbor and ends forty-two miles later at Honolulu's Ala Moana Beach Park.

AROUND LANAI

Q. What is Lanai's nickname?

A. The Pineapple Isle.

———◆———

Q. How many square miles make up Lanai?

A. 141. The island measures thirteen miles wide and eighteen miles long. It is the sixth largest Hawaiian island.

———◆———

Q. What is the tallest peak on Lanai?

A. The 3,370-foot Mount Lanaihale.

———◆———

Q. What is the official flower of Lanai?

A. The kaunaoa vine.

———◆———

Q. What is the official color of Lanai?

A. Yellow.

———◆———

Q. What two meanings does Lanai have?

A. Day of conquests—because of Lanai's ancient history, and hump or swell—reflecting the island's shape.

———◆———

Q. Where did Kamehameha the Great choose to make his summer home?

A. Kaunolu Bay.

Q. What did a Chinese immigrant on Lanai try to do with sugar cane in 1802?

A. Process sugar by crushing the cane and boiling down the syrup.

◆

Q. What did missionaries do to Hawaiian women on Maui accused of committing adultery in the 1830s?

A. Banished them to Lanai.

◆

Q. Which group first tried to farm Lanai's large flatland area, arriving in 1854 and leaving a decade later when their efforts failed?

A. Mormon missionaries.

◆

Q. What was the first town on Lanai?

A. The City of Joseph.

◆

Q. What was the name of the missionary who kept all the Mormons' landholdings on Lanai and refused to turn them over to the church in Salt Lake City?

A. Walter Gibson.

◆

Q. How did Mormon church leader Brigham Young punish Gibson?

A. He was excommunicated from the church.

◆

Q. How many Japanese laborers were brought to Lanai to work the sugarcane fields inherited by Gibson's daughter Talula Lucy in 1888?

A. More than four hundred.

◆

Q. After the sugar plantation failed, what did Talula Lucy and her husband, Frederick Hayselden, do with the land?

A. Sold it off to ranchers who formed the Lanai Company.

Q. Who purchased all but five hundred acres of Lanai in 1917?

A. The Baldwin brothers of Maui.

Q. How much did James Dole pay for the island in 1922 when he bought Lanai from the Baldwins?

A. $1.1 million ($12 an acre).

Q. In what year was Lanai City founded by James Dole?

A. 1923.

Q. How many acres of pineapple did Dole's Hawaiian Pineapple Company plant?

A. Sixteen thousand.

Q. When Dole's Hawaiian Pineapple Company lost $8 million in 1932, what company purchased most of the stock?

A. Castle & Cooke.

Q. How did the seven-mile Munro Trail receive its name?

A. For New Zealander botanist George C. Munro.

Q. What did Munro plant along the ridges above Lanai City in the early 1900s?

A. Cook and Norfolk Island pines.

Q. What sits in the Trophy Room of the Lodge at Koele?

A. A chair made completely of animal horns.

Q. How did the separated sea cliff Puupehe get its name?

A. A man was so possessive of his beautiful bride, Puupehe, that he kept her hidden from others in a cave on the sea cliff. One day, a sudden storm flooded the cave and drowned Puupehe.

Q. What did the distraught man do with Puupehe's body?

A. He built her a tomb atop the sea cliff, and then jumped to his death.

Q. In what year did the bustling Keomuku village become a ghost town?

A. In 1901, when Talula Lucy Gibson's Maunalei Sugar Company shut down.

Q. Why do Hawaiians believe the Maunalei Sugar Company failed?

A. Sacred stones from the nearby Maunalei Heiau were used to build the walls of the companies buildings.

Q. What gives Shipwreck Beach its name?

A. The rusting hull of a Liberty freighter, which ran aground during World War II on the reef off Polihua Beach.

Q. What animals were brought to Lanai specifically for hunting?

A. Axis deer and mouflon sheep.

Q. What game birds are hunted on Lanai?

A. Pheasants, quails, francolins, doves, and turkeys.

Q. Why do ground-nesting birds thrive on Lanai?

A. The island has no mongoose predators.

Q. In what country were one-third of Lanai's current residents born?

A. The Philippines.

AROUND KAHOOLAWE

Q. What is Kahoolawe's nickname?

A. The Forbidden Isle.

——————◆——————

Q. How many square miles is Kahoolawe?

A. Forty-five. The island measures eleven miles long and six miles wide. It is the smallest of the Hawaiian Islands.

——————◆——————

Q. What is the highest point on Kahoolawe?

A. Mount Lua Makika at 1,477 feet above sea level.

——————◆——————

Q. What caused Kahoolawe to lose its inhabitants in the thirteenth century?

A. A shift in climate brought little rain and created barren, uninhabitable conditions.

——————◆——————

Q. Who is the island's namesake?

A. Kanaloa, one of the four major Hawaiian gods.

——————◆——————

Q. Why did Hawaiian voyagers to Tahiti first stop at Kahoolawe?

A. In order to honor Kanaloa.

——————◆——————

Q. What does *Kealaikikahiki* (Kahoolawe's western point and channel) mean?

A. Pathway to Tahiti.

Q. What did Kamehameha III create on the island during his reign?

A. A penal colony.

—————◆—————

Q. Why was the prison soon abandoned?

A. Prisoners kept escaping to Maui and Lanai to steal food and valuables and kidnap women. They would then hijack canoes and paddle back to Kahoolawe.

—————◆—————

Q. What Hawaiian king was sent by his kahunas to Kahoolawe in 1874 to purge himself before ascending the throne?

A. King David Kalakaua.

—————◆—————

Q. Smugglers used Kahoolawe's isolated southwestern bay for what purpose?

A. To distribrute opium from Chinese ships to small, less conspicuous fishing boats.

—————◆—————

Q. Who first tried sheep ranching on the island in 1858?

A. R.C. Wyllie. He had previously developed sugar plantations at Princeville on Kauai.

—————◆—————

Q. How much did rancher Angue MacPhee charge the U.S. Navy when he subleased the southern portion of the island for target practice?

A. One dollar.

—————◆—————

Q. Who took control of Kahoolawe after the Japanese attack on Pearl Harbor?

A. The U.S. Navy.

—————◆—————

Q. What sites were immediately reduced to rubble in target practice bombings?

A. All ranch buildings and water cisterns.

Q. How much was MacPhee reimbursed for his losses?

A. Nothing.

———◆———

Q. Which islands were bombed more than Kahoolawe during World War II?

A. None. Kahoolawe was the most bombed island in the Pacific, though no enemy ever fired on it.

———◆———

Q. In what year was the entire island declared a National Historic Site?

A. 1981.

———◆———

Q. What did the U.S. Navy offer foreign nations during biennial Pacific Rim military exercises?

A. The opportunity to use Kahoolawe for bombing practice.

———◆———

Q. What countries refused due to protests from their respective environmentalist groups?

A. Britain, Japan, New Zealand, and Australia.

———◆———

Q. What destroyed most of the ground cover on the island?

A. A wild goat population that numbered in the thousands at one time. The wild goat herds have been radically reduced in recent years.

———◆———

Q. What recommendations by the 1991 Kahoolawe Island Conveyance Commission were approved by the federal government?

A. Title of the island was turned over to the state of Hawaii and a $400 million cleanup fund for the removal of unexploded shells was approved.

Q. When did the U.S. Navy formally give control of Kahoolawe back to the state of Hawaii?

A. 1994.

Q. When is it expected that Kahoolawe will be opened to the public?

A. By the year 2005. However, members of the Protect Kahoolawe Ohana currently visit the island to conduct traditional Hawaiian rituals.

AROUND THE BIG ISLAND

Q. What are the nicknames for the island of Hawaii?

A. The Big Island and the Orchid Isle.

Q. How many square miles make up the Big Island?

A. 4,038. This measurement makes it the largest of the Hawaiian Islands.

Q. How high is Mauna Kea?

A. 13,796 feet above sea level. The dormant volcano is the highest point in the Pacific.

Q. What is the second highest point in the Pacific?

A. Mauna Loa at 13,680 feet. It is also located on the Big Island.

Q. What is the official flower of the Big Island?

A. Ohia lehua.

Q. What is the official color of the Big Island?

A. Red.

Q. How old is the Big Island estimated to be?

A. It is the youngest in the Hawaiian Island chain at only about one million years old.

◆

Q. How many tourists visit the Big Island every year?

A. A little more than one million.

◆

Q. What is the tallest mountain in the world when measured from the ocean floor?

A. Mauna Kea at 33,476 feet.

◆

Q. What does *Mauna Kea* mean?

A. White mountain.

◆

Q. What is the longest ski run atop Mauna Kea?

A. Five miles.

◆

Q. What are the five volcanoes that formed the Big Island?

A. Kohala, Mauna Kea, Hualalai, Mauna Loa, and Kilauea.

◆

Q. When did Kohala last erupt?

A. Roughly sixty thousand years ago.

◆

Q. When did Mauna Kea last erupt?

A. About three thousand years ago.

Q. In what year did Hualalai last erupt?

A. 1801.

Q. In what year did Mauna Loa last erupt?

A. 1984.

Q. In what year did Kilauea begin its current activity?

A. 1983.

Q. What is the capital city of the Big Island?

A. Hilo.

Q. What makes Hilo one of the rainiest towns in the United States?

A. An average annual rainfall of 140 inches.

Q. How many days does it rain every year in Hilo?

A. Approximately 278 days.

Q. What destroyed most of Hilo's waterfront?

A. Tsunamis in 1946 and 1960.

Q. How did Rainbow Falls earn its name?

A. The sun's morning rays cast a rainbow across the pool.

Q. What does *Waianuenue*, the Hawaiian name for Rainbow Falls, mean?

A. Rainbow seen in water.

Q. Why was Coconut Island in Liliuokalani Park once called Moku Ola (Island of Life)?

A. The island has a healing stone once used by kahunas to cure the sick.

Q. What are the Naha and Pinao stones in the front lawn of the Hilo Library?

A. Pinao was part of an entrance pillar to an ancient heiau. Naha came from the same temple.

Q. Who placed the sundial inside Kalakaua Park?

A. King Kalakaua.

Q. What is the King Kalakaua statue in Kalakaua Park holding in its hands?

A. A taro leaf and a hula drum.

Q. When will the Kalakaua Park time capsule, buried on July 11, 1991, during the total solar eclipse, be opened?

A. May 3, 2106, during the next total solar eclipse over Hawaii.

Q. What currently occupies the site of Niolopa, King Kalakaua's summer home?

A. The Hilo Hotel.

Q. What is unique about Panaewa Zoo, located inside a forest reserve?

A. It is the only tropical rainforest zoo in the United States.

Q. What does the memorial in Laupahoehoe commemorate?

A. Twenty children and four teachers who were killed when a tsunami struck their school in 1946.

———◆———

Q. Why was Waipio Valley once called the Valley of the Kings?

A. It was the political center of Hawaii, with more than ten thousand residents ruled over by the most sacred chiefs and kahunas.

———◆———

Q. How many people now live in Waipio Valley?

A. About fifty.

———◆———

Q. What destroyed Waipio Valley's schools, restaurants, churches, hotel, post office, and jail in 1946?

A. A tsunami.

———◆———

Q. What is Hawaii's highest free-fall waterfall?

A. Waipio's Hiilawe Falls, with a sheer drop of more than one thousand feet.

———◆———

Q. Waipio Valley was once a training facility for what international program?

A. The Peace Corps.

———◆———

Q. Who founded the Parker Ranch in Waimea, the largest privately held ranch in the United States?

A. John Palmer Parker, a sailor from Massachusetts.

———◆———

Q. How did Parker arrive in Hawaii?

A. He jumped ship in 1809 at the age of nineteen.

Q. How did Parker acquire the land for Parker Ranch?

A. His friend Kamehameha the Great presented the land to Parker as a gift when he married one of the king's grand-daughters.

———◆———

Q. How many acres make up Parker Ranch?

A. 225,000.

———◆———

Q. How many head of cattle are on Parker Ranch?

A. More than fifty-five thousand.

———◆———

Q. When did Spanish cowboys (paniolos) arrive in Hawaii?

A. During the early 1830s.

———◆———

Q. Who brought them to Hawaii?

A. Kamehameha III, who wanted them to teach roping, riding, and herding to Hawaiians.

———◆———

Q. What artists' works can now be found in the Parker Ranch homestead, built in 1847 by John Palmer Parker?

A. Works by Chagall, Renoir, Pissarro, and Degas.

———◆———

Q. What hymn is sung in Hawaiian every Sunday at Imiola Congregational Church, built in 1830?

A. "Hawaii Aloha."

———◆———

Q. Who wrote "Hawaii Aloha"?

A. Missionary Lorenzo Lyons who served in Waimea from 1832 to 1886.

Q. Why is the Imiola Congregational Church bell kept in the garden?

A. It is too heavy for the church roof to support.

Q. Whose sacred chair is found in Kamuela museum?

A. The one belonging to Kamehameha the Great.

Q. Who oversees the Mookini Heiau in Hawi?

A. Members of the same family who have served the temple since it was built more than one thousand years ago.

Q. How much were Japanese laborers paid in 1906 to build the twenty-two-mile-long Kohala Ditch irrigation system?

A. One dollar per day.

Q. Who does the Douglas Memorial commemorate on Keanakolu Road?

A. Internationally renowned botanist David Douglas. His mysterious death on the slopes of Mauna Kea remains unsolved.

Q. What tree is named for David Douglas?

A. The Douglas fir.

Q. When was Puukohola Heiau built?

A. 1550.

Q. After supervising thousands of workers in the reconstruction of Puukohola Heiau in 1791, what did Kamehameha the Great do at the dedication?

A. Sacrifice his chief enemy, who had been invited to the ceremony.

Q. What is still visible offshore from Puukohola Heiau?

A. An underwater temple dedicated to a shark god.

——◆——

Q. Laurance Rockefeller leased the land for his Mauna Kea Beach Hotel in the early 1960s from whom?

A. Richard Smart, then owner of Parker Ranch.

——◆——

Q. How long was the term of the lease on the Mauna Kea Beach Hotel?

A. Ninety-nine years.

——◆——

Q. When the Mauna Kea Beach Hotel was completed in 1965, how many plants were brought in to landscape the surrounding barren lava fields?

A. More than five hundred thousand plants of two hundred varieties.

——◆——

Q. What is the weight of the pink granite buddha at the Mauna Kea Beach Hotel?

A. Fifteen hundred pounds.

——◆——

Q. What was the first Hawaii hotel to rank among the top three *Conde Nast Traveler* resorts in the world?

A. Ritz-Carlton Mauna Lani, now a Sheraton resort.

——◆——

Q. What historical park did the Ritz-Carlton Mauna Lani establish on its property?

A. The Puako Petroglyph Archaelogical Park. The park protects four-hundred-year-old lava rock carvings that were placed on the Hawaii and National Historic Registers in 1982.

——◆——

Q. How many carvings are found in this park?

A. More than three thousand.

Q. What was the construction cost per room when the Mauna Lani Bay Hotel was built?

A. Two hundred thousand dollars per room.

———◆———

Q. How was the Hyatt Waikoloa (now the Hilton Waikoloa) resort billed when it opened in 1988?

A. "The most expensive resort in the world," built at a cost of $360 million.

———◆———

Q. What is the value of the Pacific and Oriental art throughout the lobbies of the Hilton Waikoloa?

A. More than $3 million.

———◆———

Q. How big is the tank for the Hilton Waikoloa's Dolphin Quest?

A. 2.5 million gallons.

———◆———

Q. What is the cost per night of the Hilton Waikoloa presidential suite?

A. Three thousand dollars.

———◆———

Q. What portion of the Big Island coast receives more sunshine than any other United States coastline?

A. Keahole.

———◆———

Q. What used to stand on the site of the King Kamehameha Kona Beach Hotel?

A. The Kamakahonu residence of Kamehameha the Great, where he spent his final years ruling the Hawaiian Islands.

———◆———

Q. Where was Kamehameha the Great buried when he died in 1819?

A. He is believed to be buried in a cave near Kaloko. (This speculation was enough for Congress to declare the area a national historical park.)

Q. What was used for the mortar when building the Mikuaikaua Church in 1836?

A. Crushed then burnt coral mixed with kukui nut oil.

◆

Q. Who were some of the guests that Princess Ruth Keelikolani entertained at the Hulihee Palace in Kailua-Kona?

A. Kamehameha IV, Queen Emma, Prince Albert, King Lunalilo, and King Kalakaua.

◆

Q. Who bought Hulihee Palace when Princess Ruth died in 1883?

A. King Kalakaua.

◆

Q. What was the enormous round stone, displayed in Hulihee Palace, used for?

A. Kamehameha the Great used it as an exercise ball.

◆

Q. How many types of native Hawaiian woods were used in making Hulihee Palace's dining table?

A. Twenty-five.

◆

Q. Why were cattle regularly stampeded into Kailua Bay from 1915 to 1960?

A. To force them to swim out to waiting ships where they were hoisted aboard with slings and then shipped to Honolulu slaughterhouses.

◆

Q. How did Magic Sands Beach get its name?

A. Every spring, the sand "disappears," leaving a rocky shoreline near Pahoepahoe.

◆

Q. What does the twenty-seven-foot white pillar in the middle of Kealakekua Bay commemorate?

A. Captain James Cook, who was killed there in 1779 by angry Hawaiians.

Q. How many heiaus were once located between Kona and Kealekekua?

A. Forty.

Q. What is Kona's most famous export?

A. Kona coffee. It is grown along the upcountry slopes of Mauna Loa in the rich and porous lava-rock soil.

Q. How many Kona coffee farms are in Kailua-Kona?

A. About 650.

Q. What was Kuemanu Heiau a temple for?

A. Surfing.

Q. In ancient days, what was the only way defeated warriors could find sanctuary at Puuhonua O Honaunau (Place of Refuge) south of Kona?

A. By swimming across the bay known as the shark's den.

Q. What are the dimensions of the Great Wall barrier, built in 1550 at Puuhonua O Honaunau and still standing intact?

A. One thousand feet long, ten feet high, and seventeen feet wide.

Q. What is the Great Wall made of?

A. Lava rock. It was constructed without mortar.

Q. What is Puuhonua O Honaunau built upon?

A. A twenty-acre lava peninsula.

Q. The Keauhou Beach Hotel occupies the former site of what structure?

A. The summer cottage of Kamehameha III.

Q. Where did King Kalakaua send Robert Louis Stevenson to see a typical Hawaiian village?

A. The now nearly deserted Hookena.

Q. How many acres make up the MacFarms of Hawaii, the largest macadamia nut orchard in Hawaii?

A. Thirty-eight hundred.

Q. How many pounds of macadamia nuts are produced every year at MacFarms of Hawaii?

A. Ten million.

Q. What two Hollywood stars were original partners in Mac-Farms of Hawaii?

A. Julie Andrews and Jimmy Stewart.

Q. What is the southernmost town in the United States?

A. Naalehua.

Q. Who planted the monkeypod tree in 1866 near the Shira-kawa Motel?

A. Mark Twain.

Q. What is the southernmost point of the United States at 18.58° north of the equator?

A. Ka Lae (South Point).

Q. What event occurred at Ka Lae?

A. It is believed to be the spot where the Polynesians first landed upon discovering Hawaii in 150 A.D.

◆

Q. What color is the sand at Makahana Bay?

A. Green, due to the volcanic olivine crystals.

◆

Q. What color is the sand at Punaluu?

A. Black. This unusual sand is created when hot lava hits the ocean and breaks into fragments.

◆

Q. What is the name of the black cinder sand beach created by Kilauea's 1955 lava flows?

A. Kehena Beach in the Puna district.

◆

Q. How did kahunas trick Hawaiians into being sacrificed to the volcano?

A. By luring victims inside a Uwekahuna Bluff hut with a false floor, through which they would slip and fall into the crater below.

◆

Q. What now sits on Uwekahuna Bluff?

A. The Jagger Museum.

◆

Q. In what year was the last person killed by volcanic activity in the park?

A. 1924. A photographer was struck on the leg by a boulder from a steam explosion and bled to death.

◆

Q. What happened in 1993 when sightseers crawled past barriers to see the flow hit the ocean?

A. One fell to his fiery death, and a dozen more were hurt when a lava bench, an unstable lava crust, collapsed.

Q. How long is the completely accessible Thurston Lava Tube?

A. 450 yards. The interior ceiling ranges from ten to twenty feet above the floor.

Q. Who was the Thurston Lava Tube named for?

A. Its discoverer, Hawaii publisher Lorrin Thurston. Thurston was a strong advocate for creating a national volcanoes park.

Q. What did ancient Hawaiians use lava tubes for?

A. Burial caves.

Q. What is considered the world's most active volcano?

A. Kilauea.

Q. Kilauea has been in a state of continuous eruption since what year?

A. 1983.

Q. How many times did Kilauea erupt between 1984 and 1986?

A. Thirty times.

Q. How hot is the lava now recorded from Kilauea?

A. Greater than 2,100° F.

Q. In the past two hundred years, how many Big Island acres have been covered by lava from Kilauea and Mauna Loa?

A. More than two hundred acres.

Q. How were several hundred warriors fighting Kamehameha the Great and his army killed in 1790?

A. By the sudden eruption of Kilauea.

Q. What can still be spotted in the lava rock along the Mauna Iki Trail?

A. Footprints made by the fleeing warriors.

Q. Since 1943, what has been destroyed by the Kilauea lava flow?

A. The community of Kalapana, more than two hundred homes, churches and stores, the Queen's Bath historic site, and the picturesque Kaimu Black Sand Beach.

Q. How high were lava fountains in the 1960 eruption of Kilauea?

A. The highest were measured at around nineteen hundred feet—five hundred feet higher than the Empire State Building in New York City.

Q. How much lava poured from Kilauea every day in January 1988?

A. More than 650,000 cubic yards per day.

Q. When was the Halemaumau Crater formed?

A. In 1924, when the lava lake drained.

Q. Who trained in the Kau Desert of the Big Island?

A. Neil Armstrong and the crew of the *Apollo 11* before their historic moon walk.

Q. How did the military divert the lava flows of 1935 and 1942 that threatened Hilo?

A. By bombing the flows, redirecting the lava away from the city.

Q. How close did the 1984 Mauna Loa lava flows come to Hilo?

A. Within eight miles.

———◆———

Q. What created the Devastation Trail?

A. Kilauea's 1959 eruption.

———◆———

Q. How much lava was produced by Mauna Loa's 1950 eruption?

A. One billion tons.

———◆———

Q. Why did parishioners of the historic 1931 Star of the Sea Painted Church vote in 1990 to have the church removed from the path of a lava flow?

A. They were fearful that if it were destroyed by lava, the Catholic diocese would not build a new church.

———◆———

Q. Who do the painted murals covering the interior of Star of the Sea Painted Church memorialize?

A. Father Damien, who built Hawaii's first Catholic church in nearby Kapaahu.

———◆———

Q. How was the church moved?

A. It was separated from its foundations, hoisted onto a trailer, and towed to its current location.

———◆———

Q. What happened to the Mauna Kea Congregational Church, located across the street from the Star of the Sea Painted Church?

A. It was destroyed by lava one month after the Star of the Sea Painted Church was moved.

———◆———

Q. What heiau was spared by the 1989 eruption and by subsequent lava flows?

A. Wahaula (Red Mouth) Heiau.

Q. Why is Wahaula Heiau significant?

A. The first human sacrifices in Hawaii were performed at this Hawaiian temple.

Q. What stones were destroyed in the flow through Harry Kaina Brown Memorial Park?

A. Ancient judgement stones, to which suspected criminals were tied during their trials.

Q. What happened if those charged were found guilty?

A. The criminal was pushed into a nearby firepit.

Q. In what year was Kapoho's hot springs resort, business district, and more than one hundred homes destroyed by a lava flow?

A. 1960.

Q. The 1960 lava flow separated and rejoined around what Kapoho site?

A. Cape Kumukahi's lighthouse.

Q. During what year did lava first begin destroying homes in the Kalapana area?

A. 1983.

Q. How many cubic yards of new lava has been produced since 1943?

A. More than two billion.

Q. What happened to the Puu Oo vent in 1986?

A. The walls of the fifty-foot-wide vent collapsed and formed a crater more than five hundred feet in diameter.

Q. How many times in this century have both Kilaue Mauna Loa erupted at the same time?

A. Twice, once in 1919 and again in 1984.

———◆———

Q. Who declared Kalapana a federal disaster area in May 1990?

A. President George Bush.

———◆———

Q. When did Kalapana disappear beneath the lava flows?

A. June 1990.

———◆———

Q. What do many of the former Kalapana residents suffer from?

A. Post-traumatic stress disorder—similar to that experienced by war veterans.

———◆———

Q. Who was one of the first guests at the Volcano House in 1866?

A. Mark Twain, during his five-month visit to Hawaii.

———◆———

Q. Who is the Volcano House's Uncle George Lounge named for?

A. George Kycurgus, who owned and operated the inn from 1895 to 1960.

———◆———

Q. How did Kycurgus acquire the Volcano House in 1895?

A. He won it in a poker game.

———◆———

Q. What happened during Devastation Day in Kau on April 2, 1868?

A. An earthquake, lava flow, tsunami, and a cinder cone land-slide combined to bury an entire village.

e name of the small town within the Hawaii Vol-
tional Park?

lauea doing at a rate of several inches every year?

A. Sinking into the ocean.

AROUND KAUAI

Q. What is Kauai's nickname?

A. The Garden Isle.

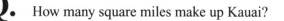

Q. How many square miles make up Kauai?

A. 558. The island measures thirty-three miles by twenty-five miles. It is the fourth largest Hawaiian island.

Q. What is the highest point on the island?

A. Mount Waialeale at 5,148 feet.

Q. What is the official flower of Kauai?

A. The mokihana blossom.

Q. What is the official color of Kauai?

A. Purple.

Q. What is the ocean depth between Oahu and Kauai?

A. 9,950 feet, the deepest channel in the Hawaiian Islands.

Q. What is the rainiest spot on earth?

A. Mount Waialeale. The mountain averages 450 to 600 inches of rain annually.

Q. What does the name Waialeale mean?

A. Overflowing water.

Q. What is the capital of Kauai County?

A. Lihue.

Q. To thwart additional high-rise development, what is Kauai's height limitation on buildings?

A. Four stories—or roughly the height of a coconut tree.

Q. What was the name of the 1992 hurricane that struck Kauai?

A. Iniki. Its winds were measured at up to 160 miles per hour.

Q. What was the estimate of damage caused by Hurricane Iniki?

A. $1.6 billion—the third costliest disaster in United States history.

Q. Who gave Waimea Canyon the nickname Grand Canyon of the Pacific?

A. Mark Twain.

Q. What is the deepest drop in Waimea Canyon?

A. 3,657 feet.

Q. What remains at Kalalau Lookout where a major settlement once stood?

A. Taro terraces and portions of a religious temple.

◆

Q. How many miles of hiking trails can be found in Kokee State Park?

A. Forty-five miles.

◆

Q. What kind of trees are clustered near Kokee State Park's Waipoo Falls?

A. California redwoods, Japanese sugai pines, and Australian eucalyptus.

◆

Q. What did Hawaiian chiefs do at Wailua Falls to prove their courage?

A. Dive off the eighty-foot waterfall.

◆

Q. What is the setting for Coco Palms Resort in Wailua?

A. A century-old grove of two thousand coconut trees planted by a German doctor.

◆

Q. Who used to live on the grounds of what is now the Coco Palms Resort?

A. Queen Deborah Kapule, wife of Kauai's last king.

◆

Q. What closed a large gap in the mountains above Anahola?

A. A landslide caused by Hurricane Iwa.

◆

Q. Where did Hawaiians harvest most of Kauai's limu kohu, the Island's famous seaweed?

A. On reefs off of Larsen's Beach.

Q. Who once owned the Princeville area?

A. Scotsman Robert Crichton Wyllie, named Hawaii's Minister of Foreign Affairs in 1789, holding the spot for more than sixty years.

———◆———

Q. For whom was Princeville named?

A. Prince Albert, heir of Kamehameha IV and Queen Emma. Wyllie renamed the town on the occasion of the prince's fourth birthday.

———◆———

Q. How much did the renovation of the Sheraton Princeville Hotel cost in 1991?

A. $120 million.

———◆———

Q. How much damage did Hurricane Iniki cause the following year to the Sheraton Princeville Hotel?

A. More than $30 million.

———◆———

Q. What is one of the areas in Hawaii settled earliest by migrating Polynesians?

A. Hanalei.

———◆———

Q. What mythical figure tried to find a home in the Waikapalae wet cave on the north coast of Kauai?

A. The fire goddess Pele.

———◆———

Q. Is the Maniniholo dry cave really a cave?

A. No, it is actually a mile-long lava tube running under a cliff.

———◆———

Q. Who first settled in the Na Pali valley in 1822?

A. The Reverend Hiram Bingham, leader of the first group of missionaries to arrive in Hawaii.

Q. What creates the blowhole effect at the Spouting Horn?

A. Waves pushing through the opening of an underwater lava tube.

———◆———

Q. Who docked at the mouth of the Waimea River in 1778?

A. Captain James Cook, on his first visit to the islands.

———◆———

Q. Who is believed to have constructed the aquaduct near the Waimea River Bridge?

A. The Menehune—Hawaii's legendary race of little people.

———◆———

Q. What is the nickname for trees with soft yellowish flowers lining Fern Grotto?

A. Scrambled egg trees.

———◆———

Q. What did Kauai Queen Deborah Kapule do to Malae Heiau when she converted to Christianity?

A. Converted the sacred site into a cattle pen.

———◆———

Q. The lei niho palaoa necklace displayed in Lihue's Kauai Museum is made of what material?

A. Strands of braided human hair.

———◆———

Q. Where were Kauai's first traffic lights installed in 1973?

A. The Rice Street intersections with Umi and Kalena Streets.

———◆———

Q. What was the interior of the 1885 Old Lutheran Church built to resemble?

A. The ship that brought German immigrants to Hawaii in the late 1800s.

Q. How much did it cost to transform the Kauai Surf Hotel into the Westin Kauai in 1987?

A. More than $350 million.

———◆———

Q. How were guests transported to the hotel's 847 rooms, 70 shops, and 16 dining rooms?

A. Either aboard one of the ninety outrigger canoes or taxied by one of the thirty-five carriages drawn by some of the one hundred purebred Clydesdales.

———◆———

Q. What sprang from the center of the hotel's 2.1-acre reflecting pool?

A. Seven galloping, white-marble horses.

———◆———

Q. How many mosaic tiles did it take to line the twenty-six-hundred-square-foot swimming pool?

A. 1.8 million.

———◆———

Q. Virtually bankrupt, what happened to the Westin Kauai in 1992?

A. It was devastated by Hurricane Iniki.

———◆———

Q. What happened to the resort?

A. It reopened in 1995 as Kauai Marriott (combination hotel and time-share) following $25 million of repairs.

———◆———

Q. What used to surround Koloa Town?

A. Hawaii's first sugar plantation, established in the 1830s.

———◆———

Q. What was Kauai's first hotel in 1898?

A. Koloa Hotel. The building is now a museum.

Q. What can scuba divers explore in waters off Koloa Landing?

A. Lava tubes and the wreck of the German freighter *Lukenbach* that sank in 1951 during a storm.

---◆---

Q. How does the Hyatt Regency Kauai heat its swimming pools and five-acre saltwater swimming lagoon?

A. By recycling heat waste from its air conditioning units.

---◆---

Q. How did Glass Beach get its name?

A. From the bits of worn glass washed ashore from an abandoned dump site.

---◆---

Q. Who had Fort Elizabeth built in 1817?

A. A German doctor named Georg Anton Scheffer.

---◆---

Q. Why was the star-shaped Fort Elizabeth named in honor of Russian Czar Nicholas's daughter?

A. With the support of Kauai King Kaumualii, Scheffer tried to convince the czar to bring Kauai and all the Hawaiian Islands under Russian rule. However, the czar was not interested.

---◆---

Q. How did Barking Sands Beach get its name?

A. The movement of the sand as waves wash back out to sea can sometimes be mistaken for the sound of barking dogs.

---◆---

Q. What is based at Barking Sands Beach?

A. The Barking Sands Pacific Missile Range. The site is home to the world's largest underwater listening device.

---◆---

Q. What company has the right to close Wahiawa Beach at any time?

A. McBryde Sugar Company.

Q. How many Hawaiians did Captain Cook estimate were living on Kauai in 1778?

A. More than thirty thousand.

———◆———

Q. According to the latest state census, how many full-blooded native Hawaiians live on Kauai?

A. Forty-six.

AROUND NIIHAU

Q. What is Niihau's nickname?

A. The Private Isle.

———◆———

Q. How many square miles is Niihau?

A. Seventy. It measures eighteen miles long by six miles wide. It is the smallest of the inhabited Hawaiian islands.

———◆———

Q. Who first owned Niihau?

A. Mrs. Elizabeth Sinclair.

———◆———

Q. How much did she pay Kamehameha V for the island?

A. Six thousand dollars.

———◆———

Q. What did Kamehameha V try to sell to Mrs. Sinclair before she purchased Niihau?

A. The marshland known as Waikiki.

———◆———

Q. What is Halalii Lake?

A. The largest lake in the islands.

Q. Niihau was the main supplier of what produce to whalers?

A. Yams. They were introduced to the island by Captain Cook's expedition in 1778.

Q. What other two things were Captain Cook and his crews the first to introduce to Hawaii on Niihau?

A. Goats and syphilis.

Q. What is the major export of Niihau today?

A. Valuable Niihau shell leis and charcoal from kiawe trees.

Q. In keeping with the 1864 wishes of its original owner, Mrs. Sinclair, what does Niihau still not have?

A. Hotels, shops, cinemas, telephones, jails, restaurants, paved roads. Only a handful of cars operate on Niihau, and there is no electricity, except at the school and the Robinson homestead.

Q. How many people now live on Niihau?

A. 230 residents.

Q. Where do residents go to drink beer, wine, and hard liquor?

A. Kauai, since Niihau is a dry island.

Q. What is the spoken language on Niihau?

A. Hawaiian.

ENTERTAINMENT

C H A P T E R T W O

Q. When the script called for silent screen legend Mary Pickford to cry, who would she hire to play "Roses of Picardy" for inspiration?

A. Hawaiian steel guitarist Solomon Hopii.

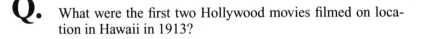

Q. Who wrote the famous "Boola Boola" college song while a student at Yale?

A. Island composer Sonny Cunha, who became known as the father of hapa-haole music.

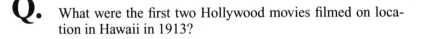

Q. The eighty-foot Wailua Falls was featured in the opening sequences of what television series?

A. *Fantasy Island.*

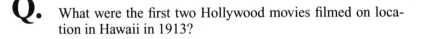

Q. What were the first two Hollywood movies filmed on location in Hawaii in 1913?

A. *Hawaiian Love* and *The Shark God.*

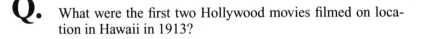

Q. What movie, filming at the time on Kauai, used actual footage of Hurricane Iniki?

A. *Jurassic Park.*

Q. What three Hawaiians are members of the Steel Guitar Hall of Fame in St. Louis, Missouri?

A. Solomon Hoopii, Dick Kaaihue, and David Kelii.

◆

Q. What was the name of "Hawaii's Songbird" of the 1930s who performed for President Franklin Roosevelt?

A. Lena Machado, who was also an accomplished songwriter.

◆

Q. What entertainer was known as Hawaii's "Queen of Comedy," famous for her comic hulas at the Kodak Hula Shows?

A. Clara Meleka Haili Inter Nelson, known professionally as Hilo Hattie.

◆

Q. Who made a 1946 slapstick hit of the "Hawaiian War Chant," composed by Prince William Pitt Kalahoolewa Leleiohoku?

A. Spike Jones, a version that hit the Top Ten.

◆

Q. Who also made hit versions of the "Hawaiian War Chant"?

A. Tommy Dorsey, Harry Owens, the Ames Brothers, and Billy Vaughn.

◆

Q. What films have featured the "Hawaiian War Chant" as part of their soundtracks?

A. *It's a Date* with Deanna Durbin (1940), *Moonlight in Hawaii* with Johnny Downs (1941), *Ship Ahoy* with Red Skelton (1942), *Song of the Islands* with Betty Grable (1942), and *Song of the Open Road* with Jane Powell (1944).

◆

Q. Who featured the song on her 1977 *Live at Last* album?

A. Bette Midler.

◆

Q. What motion picture was filmed offshore of Kawaihae?

A. The $150 million-plus *Waterworld*, starring Kevin Costner.

Q. What was the name of the Honolulu prostitute who Somerset Maugham met in Honolulu in 1916 and eventually featured in his most famous short story?

A. Sadie Thompson.

———◆———

Q. What were the three film versions of Somerset Maugham's short story?

A. *Sadie Thompson* starring Gloria Swanson (1928), *Rain* with Joan Crawford (1932) and *Miss Sadie Thompson* starring Rita Hayworth (1953).

———◆———

Q. Where was Bette Midler born?

A. At Honolulu's Kapiolani Maternity and Gynecological Hospital on December 1, 1945.

———◆———

Q. What climactic scene of a television miniseries was filmed on the cliffs above Kee Beach State Park?

A. A scene from *The Thorn Birds* in which a priest and young woman give in to their love.

———◆———

Q. Who was the inspiration for the fictional detective Charlie Chan?

A. Honolulu police detective Chang Apana.

———◆———

Q. For what purpose was the Kauai's Coco Palms Resort chapel built?

A. To serve as a backdrop for one of the scenes in the 1953 movie *Sadie Thompson*, starring Rita Hayworth.

———◆———

Q. In what other film was the Coco Palms Resort chapel used?

A. The wedding scene for *Blue Hawaii* with Elvis Presley and Joan Blackman.

———◆———

Q. What Hollywood star, while vacationing at the Moana Hotel in 1917, frequently entertained children along Waikiki Beach?

A. Charlie Chaplin.

Q. In what bar did Charlie Chan author Earl Derr Biggers supposedly meet with Apana?

A. House With a Key.

Q. What was the name of the first Charlie Chan mystery, published in 1925?

A. *House Without a Key.*

Q. What film featured the *Carthaginian*?

A. *Hawaii*, starring Julie Andrews, Richard Harris, and Max von Sydow.

Q. How old is the *Carthaginian* figurehead, which now hangs in the Lahaina Whaling Museum?

A. It was carved in 1965 for the movie *Hawaii*.

Q. Who performed at the Outdoor Circle's 1933 Community Carnival?

A. Al Jolson.

Q. In what film did Bette Midler make her motion picture debut at the age of nineteen?

A. The 1965 film *Hawaii*. She played a missionary.

Q. What Broadway star of the 1940s and 1950s also owned the Big Island's Parker Ranch, the largest private ranch in the United States at 225,000 acres?

A. Richard Smart.

Q. What Hawaii native went on to fame and fortune playing the role of Tarzan?

A. Clarence "Buster" Crabbe.

Q. Arthur Godfrey's popular radio show increased a national demand for what Hawaiian instrument?

A. The ukulele.

Q. What recording artists have homes in the Hana area of Maui?

A. Kris Kristofferson, Randy Travis, and George Harrison.

Q. What was the name of the 1930s Hawaiian female group that performed on NBC radio, at the Bing Crosby and Bob Hope golf tournaments, and for Eleanor Roosevelt?

A. The Annie Kerr Trio.

Q. What 1952 television show became the first locally sponsored program?

A. *Hopalong Cassidy*, presented by Love's Biscuit and Bread Company.

Q. Who were some of the actresses that attempted to perform the hula in movie musicals?

A. Clara Bow, Jeanette MacDonald, Dolores Del Rio, Eleanor Powell, Shirley Temple, Dorothy Lamour, and Betty Grable.

Q. Who created the popular *Hawaii Calls* radio program, which aired around the world from 1935 to 1975 with 2,082 broadcasts?

A. Corvallis, Oregon, native Webley Edwards.

Q. Who wrote *From Here to Eternity* years after being a young solider assigned to a gun emplacement at Hanauma Bay?

A. Jack Jones.

Q. What Hawaii native won an Academy Award for best song in 1980?

A. Dean Pitchford for "Fame."

Q. Who were the headliners at Hawaii's newly renamed Fiftieth State Fair in 1959?

A. Johnny Cash, Ricky Nelson, and the Kingston Trio (two of whom, Dave Guard and Bob Shane, were from Honolulu).

Q. What was the name of the Hilo police-officer-turned-songwriter best known for his song "Waikiki"?

A. Andy Kealoha Cummings.

Q. What Hawaiian tenor was "discovered" by Bob Hope in 1952, subsequently appearing with him in movies and on radio and television?

A. Alfred Aholo Apaka, who died of a heart attack in 1960.

Q. What did Hawaii tycoon Henry J. Kaiser build for Alfred Apaka?

A. His own showroom, the Tapa Room, at Kaiser's Hawaiian Village Hotel.

Q. What television series was based at Kaiser's Hawaiian Village, though it was filmed in Hollywood?

A. *Hawaiian Eye.*

Q. Who were the stars of the 1959–63 series *Hawaiian Eye*?

A. Bob Conrad, Anthony Eisley, Poncie Ponce, and Connie "Cricket" Stevens.

Q. What is the Merrie Monarch Festival?

A. A statewide hula competition.

Q. For what person is the Merrie Monarch Festival named?

A. King Kalakaua, who lifted the ban on hula in 1874.

Q. What was the original purpose of the Merrie Monarch Festival, founded in 1963?

A. To promote tourism in Hilo on the Big Island.

◆

Q. What were the two firsts ukulele virtuoso Jesse Kalima claimed in his career?

A. He was the first musician to appear live on television in Hawaii, and he was the first to amplify a ukulele.

◆

Q. How many hit records did Don Ho have?

A. One, "Tiny Bubbles."

◆

Q. How high did "Tiny Bubbles"go on the charts in 1967?

A. The song reached the number eight spot.

◆

Q. What former Hollywood stuntman and dancer on the *Ed Sullivan Show* wrote the popular songs "Ain't No Big Thing," "Days of my Youth," and "I'll Remember You"?

A. Kuioalani "Kui" Lee. He died of cancer at the age of thirty-four.

◆

Q. Haleiwa was the backdrop for what television series in 1993?

A. *Big Wave Dave's* with Adam Arkin.

◆

Q. Who has been the entertainment writer for the *Honolulu Advertiser* since 1964?

A. Wayne Harada, who actually began as a stringer for the paper in 1957.

◆

Q. How many Academy Award nominations did the film *Hawaii* receive?

A. Seven.

Q. How many Oscars did *Hawaii* win?

A. None.

Q. What was the sequel to *Hawaii*?

A. *The Hawaiians*, starring Charlton Heston.

Q. What Miss America Pageant rule did the Honolulu Junior Chamber of Commerce challenge when selecting the first Miss Hawaii in 1948?

A. Rule Seven, which allowed only whites to compete. Hawaii was granted a limited waiver allowing the territory to also enter young women of Hawaiian, Japanese, Chinese, Filipino, and/or Korean descent.

Q. Why was the first Miss Hawaii, Irmgard Waiwaole, later stripped of her title?

A. The fact was discovered that she did not finish high school—she had chosen instead to volunteer for service during World War II. Yun Tau Zane, first runner-up, went on to the Miss America competition and won Miss Congeniality.

Q. Before the category was discontinued in 1975, how many times did participants from Hawaii win Miss Congeniality in the Miss America pageant?

A. Seven.

Q. Who did the Dunes nightclub add to its staff in 1973 to attract women at lunchtime on Thursdays and Fridays?

A. Ten completely nude male servers.

Q. When did "Book 'em, Danno" become a household phrase?

A. After the *Hawaii Five-O* television series debuted in 1968.

Q. Who was the first Caucasian to win the Miss Hawaii title?

A. Jere Wright in 1956. She was a resident of Hawaii but was originally from the Mainland.

Q. What happened after Jere Wright was crowned Miss Hawaii?

A. The decision caused an uproar, with some calling for a ban against Caucasians competing in any of the local pageants.

◆

Q. Elvis and crew arrived in Hawaii in 1961 to film what movie?

A. *Blue Hawaii.*

◆

Q. What 1973 movie drew 90,000 more people than the Honolulu Symphony's 38,100 season patrons?

A. *Deep Throat* at the Queen Theater.

◆

Q. Who was the first Miss Hawaii to be awarded the Miss America title?

A. Carolyn Suzanne Sapp, Miss Hawaii 1991. She had also been Miss Diamond Head, Miss Honolulu, and Miss Kona Coffee.

◆

Q. What was the debut act for the new Honolulu International Center in 1964?

A. Jan and Dean.

◆

Q. Why was the complex later named the Neil Blaisdell Center?

A. To honor Honolulu's longtime Republican mayor.

◆

Q. What was the estimated worldwide audience for the 1973 Elvis Presley concert beamed live from Honolulu?

A. 1.5 billion.

◆

Q. Prior to 1991, how close had a Miss Hawaii gotten to the Miss America title?

A. Second runner-up Susan Dee Pickering, Miss Hawaii 1963. She was the daughter of a military family stationed on Oahu.

Q. In which East Honolulu neighborhood did Time-Life publishing magnate Henry R. Luce and his wife, Clare Boothe Luce, retire?

A. Kahala.

Q. Who was the Miss Hawaii 1978 who went on to receive an Emmy nomination for her role in the series *China Beach*, starred in *Byrds of Paradise*, and later became a successful documentary film producer?

A. Elizabeth Kupuuwailani Lindsey.

Q. What was the first satellite live-television transmission to Hawaii on November 19, 1966?

A. A college football game between Notre Dame and Michigan State. Michigan State had three Hawaii players on its team.

Q. Has a Miss Hawaii ever won the Miss U.S.A. pageant?

A. Yes. Judi Andersen captured the national crown for Hawaii in 1978.

Q. What television job did Dave Donnelly have before starting his *Honolulu Star-Bulletin* entertainment column in 1965?

A. He played Checkers on the popular kids television show *Checkers & Pogo*.

Q. Who made up two-thirds of the 1970 Hawaiian group Sunday Manoa?

A. Robert and Roland Cazimero. Peter Moon was the third member.

Q. What album receives credit for launching a renaissance of contemporary Hawaiian music?

A. *Guava Jam*, released in 1972 by Sunday Manoa.

Q. During what year did Robert and Roland form the Brothers Cazimero, which would become one of the best-selling Hawaiian groups of all time?

A. 1975.

◆

Q. How many years did the Brothers Cazimero star in their own show in the Monarch Room of the Royal Hawaiian Hotel?

A. Thirteen.

◆

Q. Who is considered the most prolific of female contemporary Island composers?

A. Irmgard Kealiiwahinealohanohokahaopuamana Aluli. She has written hundreds of Hawaiian songs without the benefit of formal music training.

◆

Q. Who is still considered Hawaii's greatest slack-key guitarist of all time?

A. Charles Philip Kunia "Gabby" Pahinui.

◆

Q. What were the ticket prices when Elvis Presley played the Honolulu Stadium in 1957?

A. $1.50 and $3.50.

◆

Q. What did Elvis Presley help build by donating his 1961 Honolulu concert proceeds?

A. The building of the USS *Arizona* war memorial in Pearl Harbor.

◆

Q. Who first recorded the song "Blue Hawaii"?

A. Bing Crosby in the 1937 film musical *Waikiki Wedding*.

◆

Q. What nightclub comic became a popular entertainment columnist for the *Honolulu Advertiser* from 1955 to 1973?

A. Eddie Sherman. His columns have been regular features in *Midweek* since 1986.

Q. During what years was the television series *Magnum PI* on the air?

A. From 1980 to 1988.

Q. Who starred as a doctor in the failed island television series *The Little People*?

A. Brian Keith.

Q. Who starred as a doctor in the failed island television series *Island Son*?

A. Richard Chamberlain.

Q. Who starred as a female investigator in the failed island television series *One West Waikiki*?

A. Cheryl Ladd.

Q. Who starred as a martial arts expert in the failed island television series *Raven*?

A. Jeff Meek.

Q. What television series moved its location from Los Angeles to Hawaii for a few seasons then returned to Los Angeles reportedly because the cost of production was too expensive in the Islands?

A. *Jake and the Fatman.*

Q. What television series star was fined thirty-five thousand dollars in 1989 for hiring illegal aliens to work at his now-closed Black Orchid restaurant?

A. Tom Selleck.

Q. Hanauma Bay's pristine beach was a backdrop for what World War II movie?

A. *From Here to Eternity.* For the passionate scene between Deborah Kerr and Burt Lancaster a small beach near the Halona Blow Hole was used.

Q. Who owned the ill-fated D.P. (Dockside Plantation) restaurant in Hawaii Kai?

A. Dolly Parton.

Q. The legend of the moo of Hanalei, Kauai, supposedly inspired what Peter, Paul, and Mary hit song?

A. "Puff, the Magic Dragon"—who "lived by the sea . . . in a land called Hana-lee."

Q. Who attempted to "wash that man right out of her hair" on Lumahai Beach?

A. Mitzi Gaynor, in the musical *South Pacific*.

Q. What doubled as Bali Hai in *South Pacific*?

A. Haena Beach.

Q. In what film did Hawaii native Tia Carrere make her feature film debut?

A. *Aloha Summer.*

Q. What 1931 movie starred Bela Lugosi and was filmed on location in Waikiki and Kailua?

A. *Charlie Chan and the Black Camel.*

Q. Coconut Island in Kaneohe Bay was used in the opening scenes of what television series?

A. *Gilligan's Island.*

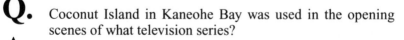

Q. Former Big Island resident Keanu Reeves returned to Hawaii to make what movie in 1990?

A. *Point Break.*

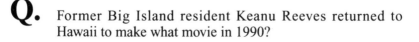

Q. George C. Scott and his three sons filmed what Ernest Hemingway classic on Kauai?

A. *Islands in the Stream.*

Q. Where was Kong captured in the 1976 remake of *King Kong* with Jessica Lange?

A. The Na Pali coast of Kauai.

Q. Kauai doubled as a remote island inhabited by shipwrecked schoolboys in what 1989 remake of William Golding's novel?

A. *Lord of the Flies.*

Q. Kauai doubled for a remote island threatened by the spread of a deadly virus in what Dustin Hoffman film?

A. *Outbreak.*

Q. What harbor is featured in the opening credits of the television series *Gilligan's Island*?

A. The Ala Wai Yacht Harbor. The SS *Minnow* departed from the harbor for a "three-hour cruise."

Q. Kauai doubled for what fantasy land in Steven Spielberg's *Hook*?

A. Never-never land.

Q. Where was Bette Midler employed while attending Radford High School and, later, the University of Hawaii?

A. KHAI radio as a secretary and at the Dole Pineapple Factory as a packer.

Q. What movie's opening scenes were filmed in Huleia National Wildlife Refuge?

A. *Raiders of the Lost Ark.*

HISTORY

C H A P T E R T H R E E

Q. When did Polynesians first settle in Hawaii?

A. Probably between 300 and 500 A.D.

Q. Where did the first settlers travel from?

A. South Pacific islands around Tahiti, including Bora Bora, Raiatea, and the Marquesas, which are more than two thousand miles to the south.

Q. Where did the name *Hawaii* come from?

A. Many believe it was adapted from the name Hawaiki, the name for a mythical homeland of all Polynesians. Others believe it is a variation of Raiatea, which was called Havaii at the time of the migration.

Q. Who introduced human sacrifice to Hawaii in the twelfth century?

A. Paao, a Tahitian priest.

Q. Who did Paao bring from Tahiti to father a royal lineage in Hawaii?

A. Chief Pili.

Q. In old Hawaii, what were women forbidden to eat?

A. Coconuts, bananas, and pork.

◆

Q. What was the Naha Stone?

A. According to legend, the Naha Stone was a forty-five-hundred-pound lava rock that could only be overturned by one who would someday rule all the islands of Hawaii.

◆

Q. Who overturned the stone?

A. Kamehameha the Great in 1775.

◆

Q. In what year did Captain James Cook "discover" Hawaii?

A. 1778. He landed at Kauai several years before Kamehameha the Great united all the islands as one kingdom.

◆

Q. What two ships were part of Captain Cook's first voyage to Hawaii?

A. The HMS *Discovery* and HMS *Resolution*.

◆

Q. Who did Hawaiians think Captain Cook was?

A. The incarnation of the god Lono.

◆

Q. What new name did Captain Cook give the Hawaiian Islands?

A. On his return visit in 1779 aboard the HMS *Discovery*, Cook named them the Sandwich Islands in honor of the earl of Sandwich and declared them part of the British Empire.

◆

Q. What precipitated Captain Cook's death in a battle on February 14, 1799?

A. Cook had attempted to take King Kalanioupuu, the uncle of Kamehameha the Great, hostage until a boat stolen from Cook's ships was returned.

Q. What did Kamehameha the Great receive for his part in the attack on Captain Cook and his men?

A. Captain Cook's scalp.

◆

Q. Over what island did Kamehameha the Great first rule as king?

A. The Big Island of Hawaii, beginning in 1790.

◆

Q. When did Kamehameha the Great conquer Maui?

A. 1790.

◆

Q. What were the names of the two English sailors who taught the warriors under the command of Kamehameha the Great how to use guns and cannons?

A. Isaac Davis and John Young.

◆

Q. Who did John Young eventually marry?

A. One of the nieces of Kamehameha the Great.

◆

Q. What gift did Vancouver give to Kamehameha the Great in 1793?

A. Cattle, the first ever brought to Hawaii.

◆

Q. Why did Kamehameha the Great forbid killing cattle, a crime punishable by death?

A. To give the cattle a chance to reproduce.

◆

Q. During what year did Kamehameha the Great conquer Oahu?

A. 1795. His victory followed two years of battles for the island.

Q. When food supplies ran short on the windward side of Oahu, what did the warriors in the army of Kamehameha the Great eat?

A. Edible mud from the Kailua marshland.

———◆———

Q. How many attempts did Kamehameha the Great make to conquer Kauai?

A. Two, in 1796 and 1804. He failed in both attempts.

———◆———

Q. When were horses first brought to the Islands?

A. In June 1803. An American merchant seaman presented a stallion and two mares as a gift to Kamehameha the Great.

———◆———

Q. Where did Kamehameha the Great rule from?

A. Waikiki and Honolulu on the island of Oahu, from 1795 to 1810.

———◆———

Q. Where did Kamehameha the Great move to?

A. Kailua-Kona on the Big Island.

———◆———

Q. Who was the favorite wife of Kamehameha the Great?

A. Kaahumanu.

———◆———

Q. Who had Kaahumanu's mother, Chieftess Namahana, been wed to twenty years earlier?

A. Kamehameha the Great. She was one of his first wives.

———◆———

Q. Who was the most sacred wife of Kamehameha the Great?

A. Keopuolani.

Q. As the highest-ranking wife of Kamehameha the Great, what were commoners forced to do as Keopuolani passed?

A. Lie prostrate on the ground.

◆

Q. Which island was Kamehameha the Great never able to conquer?

A. Kauai.

◆

Q. What did King Kaumualii of Kauai do in 1810?

A. The king offered a diplomatic surrender of the Kauai and Niihau kingdom to Kamehameha the Great.

◆

Q. The Law of the Splintered Paddle, enacted by Kamehameha the Great, declared what?

A. Random attacks on defenseless people were punishable by death.

◆

Q. What inspired the Law of the Splintered Paddle?

A. As a young man, Kamehameha the Great, with his foot caught in a crevice, was severely beaten with a canoe paddle, which eventually splintered upon impact.

◆

Q. What sacred tradition did Queen Keopuolani break in 1815 with the birth of her daughter Nahienaena?

A. Queen Keopuolani refused to give up the baby to another chief and instead chose to raise the child herself.

◆

Q. What was the name of the sailor Kamehameha the Great hired in 1815 to hunt wild cattle on the Big Island?

A. John Palmer Parker.

◆

Q. Who ascended to the throne upon the death of Kamehameha the Great in 1819?

A. Liholiho (Heaven's Great Glowing), the firstborn son of Kamehameha the Great and his most sacred wife, Keopuolani.

Q. How many wives did Kamehameha the Great have when he died?

A. Twenty-one.

Q. What did Keopuolani do the day after Kamehameha the Great died?

A. She publicly ate a coconut—a forbidden fruit for women.

Q. Liholiho was forced to share his power with whom?

A. Kaahumanu, the favorite wife of Kamehameha the Great. Once in power she appointed herself Queen Regent.

Q. Liholiho moved his capital from Kailua-Kona to what Maui town?

A. Lahaina.

Q. Acting on the advice of foreigners, how did Liholiho weaken the power of the throne?

A. By introducing a form of parliamentary government.

Q. Who was the first member of Hawaiian royalty to become a Christian?

A. High chief and royal advisor Kalanimoku. He was baptized a Catholic while aboard the visiting French ship *L'Uranie* in 1819.

Q. How many Calvinist missionaries arrived from Boston in April 1820?

A. Fourteen.

Q. How many of the first missionaries were actually ordained ministers?

A. Two, Asa Thruston and Hiram Bingham.

Q. Why did Liholiho kidnap Kauai's king, Kaumualii, and bring him to Honolulu?

A. Liholiho had heard of plans that the Kauai king was conspiring with Russian forces to overthrow his rule.

———◆———

Q. Who was Kaumualii forced to marry in 1821?

A. Queen Regent Kaahumanu.

———◆———

Q. Who did Kaahumanu also marry?

A. Kaumualii's twenty-three-year-old son, also brought to Honolulu as a royal prisoner.

———◆———

Q. Who helped the missionaries establish Christian schools and churches on the island of Kauai?

A. Deborah Kapule, favorite wife of Kauai King Kaumualii.

———◆———

Q. For what offense did the missionaries excommunicate Kapule in 1838?

A. She was caught having an affair with the young husband of one of her stepdaughters.

———◆———

Q. Who did Liholiho marry?

A. His half sister Kamamalu.

———◆———

Q. In what year did Liholiho and Kamamalu become the first Hawaiian royalty to visit another country?

A. They arrived in London in May 1824 after seven months at sea.

———◆———

Q. Before the official meeting with King George IV, Liholiho died from what?

A. Pneumonia and measles, six days after Kamamalu had died of the same.

Q. Which of Hawaii's eight monarchs reigned the longest?

A. Kauikeaouli, Kamehameha III. He ascended the throne in 1824 at the age of ten and ruled until his death in 1854.

◆

Q. Who served as advisors to the young Kamehameha III?

A. Queen Regent Kaahumanu, who died in 1832, and his half sister Kinau, until her death in 1839.

◆

Q. How did High Chieftess Kapiolani, a Christian convert, defy the gods in 1824?

A. By holding a Christian service on the rim of the Big Island's Halemaumau firepit, the home of the fire goddess Pele. (Kapiolani's niece and namesake would later become queen of Hawaii.)

◆

Q. After years of being bemused by the missionaries, in what year did Kaahumanu convert to Christianity?

A. 1825.

◆

Q. What did Kaahumanu do to support the Protestant missionaries?

A. She ordered Catholic missionaries out of the Islands in 1827. They did not return until after her death in 1832.

◆

Q. Kamehameha III owned what business by the time he was fifteen?

A. A tavern and billiard parlor.

◆

Q. What did the popular Oahu governor Boki and his wife Liliha permit in defiance of Kaahumanu?

A. They continued to allow alcohol to be sold—a violation of the queen regent's new laws of temperance.

◆

Q. Who became governor of Oahu when Boki died?

A. His widow, Liliha.

Q. During what mission was Boki lost at sea in 1829?

A. An attempt to harvest New Hebrides' sandalwood trees to use as capital in Hawaii's trade with whalers.

Q. What did Kaahumanu do to Liliha in 1831?

A. Removed her from power and gave the governorship of Oahu to Liliha's brother, Kuakini.

Q. When Kaahumanu died in 1832, who did Kamehameha III try to appoint as his new advisor?

A. The antimissionary Liliha.

Q. Who blocked the appointment?

A. Kinau, Kamehameha III's half sister and promissionary advisor, and the Council of Chiefs.

Q. How long did it take for the missionaries to create the written Hawaiian language?

A. Four years, from 1822 to 1826.

Q. In what year were the Hawaiian translations of the Old and New Testaments completed?

A. 1839.

Q. What instrument did the paniolos introduce to the Hawaiians in 1830?

A. The guitar.

Q. Where was Hawaii's first currency printed?

A. At the Lahainaluna Seminary in Lahaina on Maui. The seminary was opened in 1831.

Q. Where was Hawaii's first sugar plantation?

A. In Koloa on Kauai.

Q. When did most of the remaining royalty, including Liliha, finally convert to Christianity?

A. During the Great Revival of 1839.

Q. In what year did the Hawaiians write their first constitution, introduced by Kamehameha III and his Christian advisors one year after Hawaii's first Declaration of Civil Rights was written?

A. 1840.

Q. Who declared Hawaii under the rule of Great Britain in 1843?

A. British sea captain George Paulet.

Q. Why did Kamehameha III accept the declaration?

A. To avoid confrontation and bloodshed in his kingdom.

Q. Who did Queen Victoria send to Hawaii six months later to restore the monarchy to full authority and rule?

A. Admiral Richard Thomas.

Q. In what year did Kamehameha III move the capital from Lahaina to Honolulu?

A. 1845.

Q. What was the name of the Honolulu residence of Kamehameha III?

A. Iolani (Hawk of Heaven), built during the years of 1844 through 1846.

Q. Why was the palace torn down thirty years later?

A. To make space for a larger and grander Iolani Palace.

———◆———

Q. What did Kamehameha III give to John Parker Palmer when he married Princess Kipikane in 1847?

A. Two acres of land near Kamuela on the Big Island.

———◆———

Q. What did Kamehameha III give Princess Kipikane as her wedding gift?

A. 640 acres of land in the same area of the Big Island.

———◆———

Q. How large did the Parker Ranch eventually become?

A. 250,000 acres, making it the largest privately held ranch in the United States.

———◆———

Q. What was the Great Mahele of 1848?

A. The division of all land into three parts: a share for the common people, a share for the government, and one million acres set aside as Crown Lands—designated by Kamehameha III as his personal property.

———◆———

Q. When were foreigners allowed to own land in Hawaii?

A. Two years after the Great Mahele.

———◆———

Q. What distinctions did Honolulu receive in 1850?

A. Kamehameha III officially declared Honolulu to be a city as well as the capital of Hawaii.

———◆———

Q. What revision was made to the Hawaiian Constitution in 1852?

A. All males were given the right to vote.

Q. Due to his childless marriage, who did Kamehameha III appoint to succeed him to the throne upon his death?

A. Adopting his half sister Kinau's two sons, Kamehameha III named the younger, Alexander Liholiho, heir to the throne.

------◆------

Q. How long did Liholiho reign as Kamehameha IV?

A. Nine years, from 1854 to 1863.

------◆------

Q. Why was Kamehameha IV considered the Hawaiian Islands' first constitutional monarch?

A. He was forced to share his power with an elected Hawaii legislature.

------◆------

Q. How much money were whaling ship captains required to pay to the monarchy for every Hawaiian who joined their crew?

A. Two hundred dollars.

------◆------

Q. How did Kamehameha IV and the legislature deal with the rapid spread of leprosy in 1865?

A. By isolating those afflicted to the remote Makanalua peninsula on the northerncoast of Molokai. The leper colony became known as Kalaupapa.

------◆------

Q. Why did the missionaries ban public display or teaching of the hula in the mid-1850s?

A. The swaying of the hips during the dance was considered lewd.

------◆------

Q. Why did the missionaries ban surfing and canoeing?

A. Because parts of the body were exposed during the ocean sports.

------◆------

Q. In what year did the *Honolulu Advertiser* begin publishing?

A. 1856.

Q. What was the name of Hawaii's first female judge, appointed by Kamehameha IV?

A. Emma Metcalf Nakuina. She was judge of the Water Court and commissioner of private ways and water rights for eighteen years.

Q. What feature was added to the original Iolani Palace in 1856?

A. A flushing toilet.

Q. What local bank opened for business in 1858?

A. The Bank of Bishop & Co. It later became known as First Hawaiian Bank.

Q. Who was the godmother of Prince Albert, the only child of Kamehameha IV and his queen, Emma?

A. Great Britain's Queen Victoria.

Q. What did Kamehameha IV do after Prince Albert died at the age of four in 1862?

A. Converted to the Church of England.

Q. What was the personal goal of Queen Emma?

A. To open a hospital in Honolulu.

Q. After soliciting fourteen thousand dollars in private contributions, Queen Emma presided at the opening of what hospital in 1864?

A. The Queen's Hospital, named in her honor.

Q. Upon the death of Kamehameha IV at the age of twenty-nine, who became king?

A. His older brother, Prince Lot.

Q. How long did Prince Lot rule as Kamehameha V?

A. Nine years, from 1863 to 1872.

◆

Q. Why did Kamehameha V sell the island of Niihau to Mrs. Sinclair and her two sons in 1864 for six thousand dollars?

A. To help pull the Hawaiian government out of debt.

◆

Q. Why did Kamehameha V never marry?

A. Because of his unrequited love for his cousin Bernice Pauahi, the great-granddaughter of Kamehameha the Great.

◆

Q. Who did Bernice Pauahi choose to marry?

A. American businessman Charles Reed Bishop.

◆

Q. Who refused the request of Kamehameha V to be his heir to the throne?

A. Bernice Pauahi Bishop.

◆

Q. Who did Bernice Pauahi Bishop suggest Kamehameha V appoint as his successor instead?

A. Either Queen Emma Naea Rooke, the widow of Kamehameha IV, or Princess Ruth Keelikolani, great-granddaughter of Kamehameha the Great who had been adopted by Kaahumanu.

◆

Q. Since Kamehameha V died a bachelor and without a designated heir, what members of the Hawaiian royalty were considered by electoral chiefs for election to the throne?

A. Queen Emma, Princess Ruth, David Kalakaua—descendant of Big Island royalty who had served Kamehameha the Great, and William Charles Lunalilo, grandson of the half brother of Kamehameha the Great.

Q. Why did Queen Emma protest the election?

A. She insisted that Kamehameha IV had offered her the throne.

———◆———

Q. Who won the election in the House of Nobles balloting on January 1, 1873?

A. Lunalilo, "the Citizen King."

———◆———

Q. How long did Lunalilo reign as Kamehameha VI?

A. One year. He died of tuberculosis at the age of thirty-nine.

———◆———

Q. During Lunalilo's short reign, what was the name of the anchorage the United States wanted to purchase for a naval port?

A. Pearl River Lagoon. After its purchase, it was renamed Pearl Harbor.

———◆———

Q. What was the name of the Belgian priest who arrived in Kaulapapa on Molokai in 1873 and began caring for those stricken with leprosy?

A. Father Damien de Veuster.

———◆———

Q. When Lunalilo died a bachelor and without having named an heir, who faced off in the next election to the throne?

A. Earlier rivals David Kalakaua and Queen Emma.

———◆———

Q. What was Queen Emma's campaign slogan?

A. Hawaii for the Hawaiians.

———◆———

Q. Who won the election in the House of Nobles balloting?

A. Kalakaua, "the Merrie Monarch."

Q. How long did Kalakaua rule as king?

A. Seventeen years, from 1874 to 1891.

Q. What happened upon the announcement of Kalakaua's victory?

A. Supporters of Emma rioted in the streets of Honolulu.

Q. What did Kalakaua request of the commanding officers of American and British troops aboard warships anchored in Honolulu Harbor?

A. To send troops ashore and restore order.

Q. What was Kalakaua's profession before election to the throne?

A. He had been a lawyer since 1870.

Q. What country did Queen Emma consider Hawaii's greatest enemy?

A. The United States.

Q. Faced with a possible coup, Queen Emma offered Hawaii's surrender to what country should the United States try to seize the Islands?

A. Great Britain.

Q. Who rejected Queen Emma's proposal of surrender?

A. British Resident Commissioner James Wodehouse.

Q. Who was Kalakaua married to in 1863?

A. Kapiolani, granddaughter of the last king of Kauai.

Q. Married to Kapiolani but without children, who did Kalakaua name as his heir?

A. His younger brother, William Pitt Leleiohoku.

◆

Q. What song did Prince William compose?

A. "Hawaiian War Chant."

◆

Q. Who did Kalakaua appoint as his successor when Prince William died of rheumatic fever at the age of twenty?

A. Kalakaua's sister, Lydia Paki, who he renamed Liliuokalani.

◆

Q. What ban did King Kalakaua lift in 1874?

A. Public dancing and teaching of the hula.

◆

Q. As the first Hawaiian monarch to visit Washington, D.C., what was the purpose of King Kalakaua's 1874 visit with President Grant?

A. To secure a free-trade agreement with the United States, allowing Hawaiian-grown sugar to be shipped duty-free.

◆

Q. What did Kalakaua establish to honor his queen Kapiolani?

A. A public park named in her honor. The park was created from Crown Lands that stretched from Waikiki to the base of Diamond Head.

◆

Q. How did Kalakaua deal with severe labor shortages in the sugarcane and pineapple fields?

A. Portuguese workers were imported in 1878.

◆

Q. What did King Kalakaua become the first ruler of any kingdom to do?

A. Sail around the world.

Q. What agreement did Kalakaua and the Japanese government sign in 1885?

A. An open door policy allowing thousands of Japanese laborers to come to Hawaii.

◆

Q. What did Kalakaua provide to the United States in 1887 in exchange for renewing duty-free trade agreements?

A. Exclusive rights to Pearl Harbor and the establishment of a repair station for U.S. Navy vessels.

◆

Q. Who represented Hawaii at Queen Victoria's jubilee in London?

A. Queen Kapiolani and Liliuokalani, Kalakaua's sister and appointed heir.

◆

Q. Who did Kapiolani and Liliuokalani visit in Washington, D.C., on their return trip home?

A. President Grover Cleveland.

◆

Q. Where did the coronation of Kalakaua take place on February 12, 1883, nine years after his election to the throne?

A. At the rebuilt Iolani Palace.

◆

Q. How long did it take to construct the new $350,000 palace?

A. Three years.

◆

Q. Kalakaua was widely criticized for spending how much on his coronation ball?

A. Fifty thousand dollars.

◆

Q. King Kalakaua was a skilled player of what instrument?

A. The ukulele.

Q. What two political scandals involved Kalakaua?

A. Assertions that he was accepting bribes from opium smugglers and receiving kickbacks in exchange for arranging real estate sales.

———◆———

Q. What happened as a result of the scandals?

A. An 1887 revolt by plantation owners who refused to pay taxes to support a corrupt monarchy.

———◆———

Q. What two royal entertainment troupes were formed and sponsored by Kalakaua?

A. The Royal Hawaiian Band and the Royal Hula Troupe.

———◆———

Q. Kalakua wrote the lyrics for what anthem?

A. "Hawaii Ponoi." The kingdom's anthem remains the fiftieth state's anthem today.

———◆———

Q. Why did Germany threaten war in response to Kalakaua's efforts to form a Polynesian Confederacy?

A. Germany was trying to establish a Pacific base in Samoa. A Polynesian Confederacy would potentially forbid foreign military installations.

———◆———

Q. What was Queen Kapiolani's motto during her reign?

A. Increase the Race.

———◆———

Q. What hospital did Queen Kapiolani found?

A. Kapiolani Maternity Hospital.

———◆———

Q. How did the Hawaiian League, a political organization of sugar plantation barons, succeed in weakening Kalakaua's powers?

A. By forcing Kalakaua to appoint a new cabinet without native Hawaiian members that was to act independently of the king.

Q. Why did Kalakaua agree to the Hawaiian League's terms?

A. The league had formed an army ready to overthrow the monarchy if the king failed to submit.

Q. What was *Paradise of the Pacific*?

A. A magazine founded by Kalakaua in 1888, which continues to publish today as *Honolulu Magazine*.

Q. Why did Kalakaua travel to San Francisco in late 1890?

A. To seek better medical attention for his declining health.

Q. What happened as soon as King Kalakaua arrived in San Francisco in January 1891?

A. He suffered a stroke and kidney failure and died at age fifty-four in his room at the Palace Hotel.

Q. Who was Hawaii's eighth and final monarch?

A. Liliuokalani. She was also Hawaii's first and only ruling queen.

Q. To whom was Liliuokalani engaged for a short time?

A. William Lunalilo, who would later become Hawaii's first elected king.

Q. Who did Liliuokalani eventually marry in 1862?

A. John Owen Dominis, the son of an Italian sea captain.

Q. Where did the couple live before moving to Iolani Palace?

A. In the Dominis home, Washington Place, a few blocks from the palace.

Q. What tragedy struck Liliuokalani a few months into her reign?

A. Her husband, Prince Consort John Owen Dominis, died.

◆

Q. Who did Liliuokalani name as heir to the throne?

A. Her niece, Princess Victoria Kaiulani.

◆

Q. Who was the half-Hawaiian politican from Maui who in 1892 denounced Liliuokalani's rule by proclaiming, "I do not wish to be governed by dolls. I believe no woman ought to reign"?

A. Robert William Wilcox.

◆

Q. On what charge was Wilcox arrested?

A. Conspiracy against the queen. His case never came to trial.

◆

Q. Who was Liluokalani's most vocal opponent?

A. Lorrin Thurston, a missionary descendant, who opposed the queen's plan to create a new constitution and restore power to the monarchy.

◆

Q. What secret political organization was led by Lorrin Thurston?

A. The Annexationist Club.

◆

Q. Which president was the first to support the idea of making Hawaii an annex of the United States?

A. Benjamin Harrison.

◆

Q. What was the purpose of the Annexationist Club's Committee of Safety?

A. To serve as a provisional government after the overthrow of the Hawaiian monarchy.

Q. What did Queen Liliuokalani's new handpicked cabinet refuse to do on January 14, 1893?

A. Dissolve the legislature and proclaim a new constitution restoring absolute power to the Hawaiian monarchy.

Q. On what date did Liliuokalani, under protest, resign her throne to the Annexationist Club's thirteen-member Committee of Safety?

A. January 17, 1893.

Q. What order did Hawaii's American Minister John Stevens give to American troops in the Islands?

A. The order to support Hawaii's new provisional government.

Q. Who became president of the provisional government?

A. Sanford Dole, son of a missionary.

Q. How did Princess Victoria Kaiulani, heir to the throne, hear of the overthrow?

A. She received a telegram while attending a girl's boarding school in England.

Q. How did the provisional government replace them?

A. By hiring thirty-five Caucasian musicians from the Mainland.

Q. What did Kaiulani's father, successful Hawaii businessman Archibald Cleghorn, propose to Lorrin Thurston's Committee of Safety?

A. In an effort to save the monarchy, Cleghorn offered his well liked daughter as an appropriate queen and legitimate substitute to Liliuokalani.

Q. Why did President Cleveland send special commissioner James H. Blount to Hawaii after meeting with Princess Kaiulani?

A. To review how the United States government might aid in the restoration of the monarchy.

Q. What conclusion did Blount make in his report to President Cleveland concerning the overthrow?

A. That Liliuokalani had a legitimate right to the Hawaiian throne, and that the overthrow was the result of unauthorized actions by American Minister Stevens.

Q. What conditions did Liliuokalani refuse to accept that would have allowed the United States to intervene as mediator and try to restore the queen to the throne?

A. General clemency for all involved in the overthrow.

Q. What did Liliuokalani propose instead?

A. Exile for all involved in the overthrow.

Q. How were native Hawaiians depicted in political cartoons published across the country at the time?

A. As Africans with bare feet, rings in their noses, and corn row hair.

Q. Who submitted a report to the United States Senate supporting the provisional government's actions?

A. Alabama senator John Tyler Morgan.

Q. After the United States Senate failed to approve annexation of Hawaii, what did Sanford Dole do?

A. Declared the Islands the Republic of Hawaii on July 4, 1894.

Q. Who led the brief January 1895 counterrevolution to restore the monarchy?

A. Former dissident Robert Wilcox and Liliuokalani's nephew Prince Jonah Kuhio Kalanianaole.

Q. Why was Liliuokalani arrested on January 16, 1895, almost two years after abdicating her throne?

A. The former queen was implicated in the counterrevolution when guns and ammunition were found buried in the gardens of her Washington Place residence.

Q. Where was Liliuokalani held prisoner?

A. In a small corner apartment on the second floor of Iolani Palace.

Q. To what name was Liliuokalani forced to answer during her trial?

A. As Mrs. Dominis.

Q. How did Liliuokalani formally abdicate the throne on January 24, 1895?

A. By signing a document renouncing any claim to the throne and recognizing the provisional government as the legitimate heir to the monarchy.

Q. What was Liliuokalani's sentence after she was tried and found guilty of treason?

A. Five years of hard labor and a five-thousand-dollar fine.

Q. Who commuted Liliuokalani's sentence?

A. Hawaii President Dole.

Q. How long was Liliuokalani kept under house arrest following Dole's commutation of her sentence?

A. Seven months.

Q. When did Liliuokalani receive a full pardon?

A. 1896.

Q. Of her many compositions, Liliuokalani is best remembered for writing what Hawaiian song?

A. "Aloha Oe."

Q. Who sent a crew in 1898 from his film company to shoot Hawaiian scenes in the Islands?

A. Thomas Edison.

Q. In what year did the United States Congress vote to annex Hawaii?

A. 1898.

Q. What caused the death of Princess Kaiulani in 1899 at the age of twenty-three?

A. Rheumatism. However, many still say she died of a broken heart at the loss of her beloved Hawaii.

Q. Who was the first woman to openly teach the hula again?

A. Isabella Kalili Desha. She had secretly danced and taught for years during the missionaries' ban of the traditional Hawaiian dance.

Q. What did Congress vote to declare in 1900?

A. Hawaii as a territory of the United States.

Q. Who was the first Hawaii representative to the United States Congress once the Territory of Hawaii was approved?

A. Robert Wilcox, serving from 1900 to 1902.

Q. Who was the first governor of the Territory of Hawaii?

A. Former Republic of Hawaii president Sanford Dole.

Q. Who was elected Hawaii representative to the United States Congress in 1902, serving for ten two-year terms?

A. Liliuokalani's nephew, Prince Jonah Kuhio Kalanianaole.

◆

Q. How did Liliuokalani spend the rest of her life?

A. Lecturing throughout the United States against the overthrow of her monarchy.

◆

Q. What was the name of Liliuokalani's autobiography?

A. *Hawaii's Story by Hawaii's Queen*. It is still in print today.

◆

Q. In what year did Liliuokalani die at the age of seventy-eight?

A. 1917.

◆

Q. What did Liliuokalani do with the Hawaiian flag just a few months before her death?

A. She asked that the Hawaiian flag finally be lowered and the American flag raised over her Washington Place residence.

◆

Q. In what year did a group of small dairies form the Honolulu Dairymen's Association?

A. 1897. Nine decades later, the group became Meadow Gold Dairies of Hawaii and was purchased by Borden in 1986.

◆

Q. What was the first automobile in Hawaii?

A. A Wood Electric. It arrrived on October 8, 1899, purchased by H.A. Baldwin of Honolulu.

◆

Q. What delivery service began in 1901?

A. Mail carrier service.

Q. When did the Moana, Hawaii's first resort, open?

A. March 11, 1901. The first guests arrived aboard the SS *Sierra*.

◆

Q. What is the Moana's nickname?

A. The First Lady of Waikiki.

◆

Q. When did James Dole found the Hawaiian Pineapple Company?

A. 1901.

◆

Q. Who was paid by a group of businessmen in 1902 to travel to the United States and show "stereopticon" pictures of Hawaii, encouraging Mainland audiences to visit the Islands?

A. W.C. Weedon. He was backed by the Hawaii Promotion Committee.

◆

Q. Who was appointed as one of Hawaii's delegates to the United States Congress?

A. Prince Jonah Kuhio Kalanianaole.

◆

Q. What link to the Mainland was completed in 1902?

A. The transpacific cable between San Francisco and Honolulu.

◆

Q. Where was Hawaii's first motion picture theater built?

A. The Orpheum was Hawaii's first motion picture theater and was located on Fort Street.

◆

Q. Founded in 1903, the Daughters of Hawaii sought to achieve what goals?

A. To perpetuate the memory and spirit of old Hawaii as well as its historic facts and to preserve correct pronunciation of the Hawaiian language.

Q. The first transpacific yacht race was held in 1906 between which two cities?

A. Los Angeles and Honolulu.

Q. Formed in 1908, what was the name of Hawaii's first industrial union?

A. The Higher Wages Association.

Q. What percent of Hawaii's population was Hawaiian in 1910?

A. 14 percent.

Q. What was the name of the first warship to dock at Pearl Harbor?

A. The USS *California*, arriving in 1911.

Q. How many miles of paved road did Hawaii have in 1912?

A. About 170. There are 1,444 miles of paved roads today.

Q. How many licensed automobiles were in Hawaii in 1912?

A. Nine hundred. There are more than six hundred thousand licensed cars today.

Q. In 1914, what was the first cargo to pass through the new Panama Canal ?

A. A bargeload of sugar from Hawaii.

Q. What record sailing time was set by the SS *Great Northern* travelling between Honolulu and San Francisco in 1915?

A. Three days, eighteen hours, and fifty-one minutes.

Q. What F-4 submarine sank in Honolulu harbor in 1915?

A. The Skate. All twenty-one aboard perished.

Q. What "first" occurred between Honolulu and Molokai on March 15, 1918?

A. The first interisland flight, completed by Major Harold Clark.

Q. What was the organization that successfully drove all billboard companies out of Hawaii by 1927?

A. The Outdoor Circle, a beautification group founded by women in 1912.

Q. What is *Hawaii Hochi*?

A. A Japanese newspaper founded on December 7, 1912 by Fred Kinzaburo Makino, the son of a British merchant father and a Japanese mother. The paper continues to print today in both English and Japanese.

Q. How long did the body of Queen Liliuokalani lie in royal state in Kawaihao Church upon her death in 1917?

A. One week. Hawaiian custom called for a twenty-four-hour death watch by attendants.

Q. Who would have been the next ruler of Hawaii if the monarchy had still existed?

A. Hawaii's congressional representative, Prince Jonah Kuhio Kalanianaole. He became heir to the throne after the death of his cousin, Princess Kaiulani, in 1899.

Q. What formally opened at Pearl Harbor in 1918?

A. The dry dock.

Q. What bill was first proposed to Congress by Hawaii representative Prince Jonah Kuhio Kalanianaole in 1919?

A. Statehood for Hawaii.

Q. During the 1920s, what was dumped into Waikiki marshlands by the tons to turn the wet land into dry?

A. Coral.

Q. A 1921 edition of the magazine *Paradise of the Pacific* predicted that in the near future what would surpass sugar and pineapples as Hawaii's number one "crop"?

A. Tourists.

Q. Who was given the last burial ceremony for royalty in Hawaii when he died in 1922?

A. Prince Jonah Kuhio Kalanianaole. He had been Hawaii's congressional representative for twenty years and heir to the throne.

Q. Who was the first woman to hold public office in the Hawaii Territory?

A. Rosalie Keliinoi. She was elected to the House of Representatives in 1924.

Q. What was Keliinoi's greatest accomplishment during her single term as a representative?

A. Granting women the right to buy, own, and sell property.

Q. In what year did Waikiki's second luxury resort, the Royal Hawaiian Hotel, open for business?

A. The hotel opened for guests and residents in 1927.

Q. How much did it cost Matson Navigation Company to build the Royal Hawaiian Hotel?

A. $3 million.

Q. What was the the Royal Hawaiian Hotel's nickname?

A. The Pink Palace of the Pacific.

◆

Q. Why was Honolulu's first civilian airfield named for Commander John Rodgers in 1928?

A. He had attempted to pilot a navy seaplane from the Mainland to Hawaii in 1925, running out of fuel three hundred miles from the Islands. He and his crew drifted for nine days before being rescued off Kauai.

◆

Q. Movies with sound came to Hawaii in 1929, with the first regular showings at what downtown theater?

A. Hawaii Theater.

◆

Q. What fashionable San Francisco boutique opened a Waikiki location in 1929?

A. Gump's.

◆

Q. What was the first interisland airline service?

A. Hawaiian Airways was the first, beginning service on November 9, 1929, two days before Interisland Airlines started service. Hawaiian Airways bankrupted in two months, and Interisland Airlines eventually became Hawaiian Air.

◆

Q. The first commercial radiotelephone service connected Hawaii and what other city?

A. London.

◆

Q. Where did Dole first introduce pineapple juice to Americans?

A. At the 1933 Chicago World's Fair.

◆

Q. In 1935, Hawaii paid more taxes to the federal treasury than how many states?

A. Sixteen. This fact pompted another plea for statehood consideration.

Q. What drainage canal was built in 1919 to combat health hazards caused by neglected fish ponds?

A. The Waikiki Canal. It was later renamed the Ala Wai Canal.

Q. How many men in the Hawaii Territory registered for Selective Service in 1940?

A. 60,136.

Q. Who was the aviator to make the first 1935 transpacific flight from Hawaii?

A. Amelia Earhart.

Q. After several years in commission, the cruiser *Honolulu* visited what city for the first time in 1938?

A. Honolulu.

Q. How many Japanese planes were involved in the December 7, 1941, surprise attack on Pearl Harbor?

A. 360.

Q. How many Americans were killed in the attack?

A. 3,435.

Q. How many Japanese were killed?

A. 100.

Q. What was the name of the American freighter hit by a Japanese submarine torpedo about one thousand miles northeast of Oahu on December 7, 1941?

A. SS *Cynthia Olson*.

Q. Who placed Hawaii under martial law by midday on December 7, 1941?

A. Gov. Joseph Poindexter.

◆

Q. Who assumed control of the territorial government at the request of Governor Poindexter?

A. Maj. Gen. Walter Short, commanding general of the Hawaiian Military Department.

◆

Q. Why was a defensive position established at Hanauma Bay on Oahu?

A. The navy viewed it as a perfect landing site for the Japanese army.

◆

Q. What was Hanauma Bay's code name?

A. Minnesota Beach.

◆

Q. Who was kept at Sand Island Detention Center internment camps from December 1941 to March 1943?

A. Island residents of Japanese, German, Italian, and Austrian descent.

◆

Q. During World War II, what resort hotel became a navy R & R retreat?

A. The Royal Hawaiian Hotel.

◆

Q. What did the Waialae Golf Club become?

A. An army recreation center. The club is now home to the Hawaiian Open.

◆

Q. During World War II, what were Honolulu nightspots forbidden to serve from 6 to 9 P.M.?

A. Liquor.

Q. What was Hawaii's curfew time during World War II?

A. 10 P.M.

Q. How many Honolulu prostitutes registered as "entertainers" with the Honolulu Police Department during the war?

A. More than 250.

Q. What establishments were closed in Honolulu in 1944?

A. Brothels. Hawaii's divorce rate had climbed to three times that of the Mainland.

Q. In 1945, Hawaii made a bid to become the home of what international organization?

A. The United Nations.

Q. Two Honolulu public school teachers were fired in 1948 for being members of what political party?

A. The Communist Party.

Q. What did the Hawaii Bar Association vote in 1949?

A. To expel all members suspected of being communist sympathizers.

Q. What was dedicated in 1949?

A. The National Memorial Cemetery of the Pacific in Punchbowl Crater.

Q. How much did Matson Lines charge for a round-trip cruise aboard the SS *Lurline* in the early 1950s?

A. $260.

Q. What did the 1950 House Un-American Activities Committee assert had happened to Hawaii's labor unions?

A. That they were under communist control.

———◆———

Q. How was Honolulu finally connected to the windward side of Oahu in 1957?

A. With the Nuuanu Pali Highway tunnels. The tunnels were constructed in less than two years for $3 million.

———◆———

Q. What was the Statehood Roll of Honor?

A. A three-mile-long petition for statehood containing approximately 150,000 signatures.

———◆———

Q. What became of the Statehood Roll of Honor?

A. It was rolled and shipped to Congress in 1954.

———◆———

Q. What bill did Congress reject in 1955?

A. An Alaska-Hawaii joint statehood bill. Alaska would finally win statehood in 1958.

———◆———

Q. How many congressional hearings on Hawaii statehood were held?

A. Thirty-four.

———◆———

Q. When did the United States Senate pass the Hawaii statehood bill?

A. March 11, 1959.

———◆———

Q. When did the House pass an identical bill?

A. The following day.

Q. When did President Eisenhower sign the bill into law?

A. March 18, 1959.

Q. Who led the formal procession to Kawaiahao Church to give thanks that Congress had passed the statehood bill?

A. Champion surfer and 1912 Olympic gold medalist Duke Kahanamoku.

Q. How did the citizens of Hawaii vote on the admission referendum in June 1959?

A. 132,938 in favor and 7,854 opppposed.

Q. What was the only Hawaii precinct to reject the statehood referendum?

A. Niihau, the privately owned island off Kauai with a population primarily made up of citizens of Hawaiian descent.

Q. When did Hawaii officially become the fiftieth state?

A. August 21, 1959. The proclamation was signed by President Eisenhower at 4 P.M. eastern time.

Q. Who was the first elected governor of the state of Hawaii?

A. Incumbent Hawaii Territory Governor William Quinn.

Q. Who did Quinn defeat?

A. Democrat Jack Burns.

Q. What hurricane caused major damage to Hawaii in 1959?

A. Dot.

Q. What Big Island village was completely destroyed by Kilauea's 1960 eruption?

A. Kapoho.

Q. How many tourists visited Hawaii in 1960?

A. About three hundred thousand.

Q. How many people were killed in the 1960 tsunami that destroyed part of Hilo on the Big Island?

A. Sixty-one.

Q. Who was the first known swimmer to complete the treacherous twenty-mile Molokai Channel?

A. Schoolteacher Keo Nakama in 1961. He swam the channel in fifteen hours and thirty-seven minutes while protected by a shark cage.

Q. Who was elected governor in 1962?

A. Jack Burns. His political career would include three terms as governor of Hawaii.

Q. How many times did President Lyndon Johnson travel to Hawaii from 1966 through 1968 for meetings with South Vietnamese leaders?

A. Six.

Q. During what year did Hawaii's visitor count top one million?

A. 1967.

Q. When did the first McDonald's restaurant open in the Aina Haina area of Honolulu?

A. 1968. (Hamburgers could be purchased for 23¢.)

Q. Of Hawaii's forty-six hundred army reserves and national guardsmen who were called up for active duty in Vietnam in 1968, how many signed a protest petition?

A. Fifteen hundred.

Q. When the *Apollo 11* crew was brought to Honolulu following their splashdown in the Pacific, how many residents turned out to greet them?

A. Twenty-five thousand.

Q. Who entertained the astronauts and crowd?

A. Don Ho.

Q. Who gave his seven-acre Kauai beachfront estate to hippies to use as a commune in 1969?

A. Howard Taylor, brother of actress Elizabeth Taylor.

Q. In 1970, Hawaii became the first state to legalize what controversial procedure?

A. Abortion.

Q. How many tourists visited Hawaii in 1972?

A. Two million.

Q. Hawaii became the first state to pass what proposed amendment in 1972?

A. The Equal Rights Amendment.

Q. What items were added to the Islands' McDonald's menu that helped the locations outperform the average Mainland McDonald's?

A. Portuguese sausage, eggs-and-rice breakfast platters, saimin, and guava juice.

Q. Who was the first Japanese American elected governor of a state?

A. Hawaii governor George R. Ariyoshi, elected in 1974.

Q. Who was elected Hawaii's first female lieutenant governor in 1978?

A. Jean King.

Q. What series of events caused President Gerald Ford to declare Hawaii a major disaster area in 1975?

A. Weeks of earthquakes, tsunamis, and volcanic eruptions.

Q. How many tourists visited Hawaii in 1976?

A. Three million.

Q. How many tourists visited Hawaii in 1979?

A. Almost four million.

Q. Who defeated longtime Honolulu mayor Frank Fasi in 1980?

A. Eileen Anderson.

Q. What was the name of the 1982 hurricane that severely damaged Oahu and Kauai?

A. Iwa.

Q. In 1982, what did *Newsweek* report as Hawaii's number one revenue producing crop?

A. Marijuana.

Q. What was the annual revenue for Hawaii's marijuana sales reported to be?

A. More than one-half billion dollars. This figure is followed by revenues from the sale of sugar at $352 million and from the sale of pineapple at $206 million.

◆

Q. During what year did Hawaii's population top one million?

A. 1983.

◆

Q. Who defeated Eileen Anderson to become mayor of Honolulu in 1984?

A. Denmocrat-turned-independent-turned-Republican Frank Fasi.

◆

Q. Who was the first person of Hawaiian ancestry elected governor of Hawaii?

A. Democrat John Waihee in 1986.

◆

Q. What did Hawaii outlaw in 1989 to protect the earth's ozone layer?

A. Chlorofluorocarbon refrigerants.

◆

Q. What was the total number of tourists who visited Hawaii in 1995?

A. More than six million.

◆

Q. Who enacted 1993 legislation to return Kahoolawe to the state?

A. President Bill Clinton.

◆

Q. What does the upside-down Hawaiian flag symbolize?

A. The Hawaiian sovereignty movement.

Q. What did Ka Lahui Hawaii adopt on the centennial of the overthrow of the Hawaiian monarchy?

A. A constitution for a Hawaiian nation within the United States.

Q. Ka Lahui Hawaii based its constitution on what?

A. The more than three hundred Native American groups that have governments that rule over their own tribal lands.

Q. What did President Clinton do in November 1993?

A. He signed a resolution apologizing to Hawaiians for the overthrow of the monarchy—an action that was done with "the participation of agents and citizens of the United States."

Q. How many sovereignty groups are there?

A. About fifty.

Q. What are some of the demands of the sovereignty groups?

A. Self-rule, restoration of the monarchy, financial reparations, and the return of more than 1.7 million acres of land to the Hawaiian people.

Q. What commission was formed to unite the sovereignty groups?

A. The Hawaiian Sovereignty Advisory Commission.

Q. What percent of Hawaii residents favor the commission's plebiscite to form a nation-within-a-nation for Hawaiians?

A. 70 percent.

Q. Who would be ruler should the Hawaiian monarchy be restored?

A. Either Abigail Kinoiki Kekaulike Kawananakoa or her first cousin, Edward Kawananakoa, since both trace ancestry back to Kamehameha the Great.

———◆———

Q. How many residents moved away from Hawaii in 1995?

A. More than twelve thousand—twice as many as moved to the Islands during the same period.

CULTURE OF THE ISLANDERS

C H A P T E R   F O U R

Q. When is the pidgin (Hawaii's broken form of English) phrase *da kine* used?

A. Whenever you can't think of a word but the listener knows what you mean.

———◆———

Q. What is the nickname for the state of Hawaii?

A. The Aloha State.

———◆———

Q. When was the state flag designed?

A. In 1816 for the united kingdom of Kamehameha the Great.

———◆———

Q. In addition to the British Union Jack, what do the eight red, white, and blue stripes represent on the flag?

A. The eight major islands of Hawaii.

———◆———

Q. What cultures are represented in Kepaniwai Park's Heritage Gardens on the island of Maui?

A. Hawaiian, Chinese, Japanese, Portuguese, and Filipino.

Q. How many native Hawaiians were living at the time of King Kalakaua's reign in the 1870s?

A. An estimated five hundred thousand.

———◆———

Q. How many native Hawaiians are living today?

A. Fewer than nine thousand.

———◆———

Q. What ethnic group in Hawaii has the lowest median family income?

A. Native Hawaiian.

———◆———

Q. What percent of Hawaii's population is Hawaiian?

A. 6 percent.

———◆———

Q. What percent of Hawaii's prison inmates are Hawaiian?

A. 40 percent.

———◆———

Q. How many native Hawaiians will be living in the year 2045, according to the University of Hawaii Center for Hawaiian Studies?

A. None.

———◆———

Q. Who jumped ship in 1848 and worked at a Honolulu bowling alley?

A. Herman Melville, author of *Moby Dick*.

———◆———

Q. What does *haole* mean?

A. Caucasian.

Q. How many trees have been planted by the Outdoor Circle, Hawaii's beautification organization founded in 1912?

A. More than five hundred thousand.

———◆———

Q. What powerful eight-term president of the Outdoor Circle also founded many of Hawaii's first recycling programs in the 1970s and 1980s?

A. Betty Crocker.

———◆———

Q. What does *mahalo* mean?

A. Thank you.

———◆———

Q. How much is Hawaii's per capita appropriations for state arts and entertainment agencies?

A. About $7.50. This figure is the highest in the nation, well above the $1 national average.

———◆———

Q. How many Islanders work for the state?

A. Approximately one in every twenty-two.

———◆———

Q. What is the average life expectancy in Hawaii?

A. Seventy-seven years—compared to the national average of seventy-three years.

———◆———

Q. How are "man," "woman," and "child" expressed in Hawaiian?

A. *Kane*, *wahine*, and *keiki*.

———◆———

Q. What Hawaii businessman broke the record in 1989 for a catamaran trip from San Pedro, California, to Diamond Head?

A. Rudy Choy (twenty-two hours, forty-one minutes, and twelve seconds).

Q. Who was the Hawaii businessman who set a powerboat record in 1989 from New York Harbor to England?

A. Tom Gentry (sixty-two hours and seven minutes).

Q. What is the English translation of *wikiwiki*?

A. Fast, quick.

Q. What is pidgin for "surfboard"?

A. *Stick.*

Q. What is the male-to-female ratio among Hawaii's residents?

A. Approximately 104 males to 100 females.

Q. What is Honolulu's record low temperature?

A. Fifty-three degrees.

Q. Hawaii has the fastest growing rate in the nation of what social malady?

A. Teen suicide.

Q. What does one in every twenty Hawaii residents suffer?

A. Depression.

Q. Who said "Hawaii has always been a very pivotal role in the Pacific. It is in the Pacific. It is part of the United States that is an island that is right here"?

A. Vice President Dan Quayle during a visit to Honolulu in 1989.

Q. What does *lolo* mean?

A. Crazy, stupid.

◆

Q. What was the longest lei ever made?

A. 14,500 feet long. This lei was made of paper flowers and dedicated in 1994 to victims of Hurricane Iniki.

◆

Q. In 1990, how much did a Japanese corporation pay for all fifty-eight of Hawaii's 7-Eleven stores?

A. $75 million.

◆

Q. How much higher is the cost of living in Hawaii than that of the Mainland?

A. Approximately 25 percent more.

◆

Q. What does a 1912 law require all cats and dogs to undergo upon arriving in Hawaii?

A. A 120-day quarantine at the state animal quarantine station in Halawa.

◆

Q. How many miles of beachfront property are there in Hawaii?

A. Fifty-six.

◆

Q. How many acres of beaches are there in Hawaii?

A. 490.

◆

Q. Who owns the beaches in Hawaii?

A. The state government. All beaches are considered public domain.

Q. What does the pidgin phrase *fo' real* mean?

A. Really? I can't believe it. Wow!

Q. What 26.2-mile roadway was deemed obsolete when it was officially finished in 1986?

A. Hawaii's first interstate, H-1.

Q. What does *holoholo* mean?

A. To travel around, go exploring.

Q. What is the most expensive private school in the Islands?

A. Punahou School. Tuition for Punahou is more than eight thousand dollars per year.

Q. What does *akamai* mean?

A. Smart, clever.

Q. What are two directions common on all of the Islands?

A. Mauka (toward the mountains, center of the island) and makai (toward the sea).

Q. During what year did Ferdinand Marcos and his wife Imelda move to Honolulu after being exiled from the Philippines?

A. 1986.

Q. What is the pidgin word for "stealing"?

A. *Cockaroach.*

Q. What is the longest first name on a Hawaii birth certificate?

A. Keliihokulanileikulamakakeanuenueohaleakala with forty-three letters.

———◆———

Q. What is the shortest last name on a Hawaii birth certificate?

A. I.

———◆———

Q. Hawaii ranks number one in the consumption of what processed meat, with four out of every one hundred cans produced eaten in the Islands.

A. Spam.

———◆———

Q. What does the pidgin phrase *broke da mouth* mean?

A. Delicious.

———◆———

Q. Who was the first American of Japanese ancestry elected to the United States Senate?

A. Daniel K. Inouye.

———◆———

Q. Who was the first woman of Japanese ancestry elected to Congress in 1964?

A. Patsy Mink from Maui.

———◆———

Q. Who was the first Chinese American elected to the United States Senate?

A. Hiram Fong.

———◆———

Q. Who was the first person of Hawaiian ancestry elected to Congress?

A. Daniel Akaka.

Q. Who was the first female mayor of Kauai County?

A. JoAnn Yukimura.

Q. Who was the first female mayor of Maui County?

A. Linda Crocket Lingle.

Q. Who was the first female mayor of the Big Island County?

A. Lorraine Inouye.

Q. Who was the first and only Republican senator from Hawaii?

A. Hiram Fong.

Q. Who was the first and only Republican member of the House of Representatives from Hawaii?

A. Patricia Saiki.

Q. Who chaired the Iran-Contra investigation committee?

A. U.S. Sen. Daniel K. Inouye of Hawaii.

Q. Who was Gov. George Ariyoshi's Japanese-American running mate in 1974?

A. Nelson Doi.

Q. Who was Governor Ariyoshi's female running mate in 1978?

A. Jean King.

Q. Who was Governor Ariyoshi's Hawaiian running mate in his third and final successful bid for reelection in 1982?

A. John Waihee.

Q. How many Republican governors have been elected since statehood?

A. One, Governor Quinn in 1960.

Q. What does *kokua* mean?

A. Help, cooperate.

Q. Where did Mark Chapman buy the gun with which he killed John Lennon in 1980?

A. A Young Street gun shop in Honolulu.

Q. Who was the Hawaii astronaut killed in the *Challenger* space shuttle disaster?

A. Ellison Onizuka from Kona.

Q. Who attended Onizuka's Buddhist burial in June 1986 at the National Cemetery of the Pacific?

A. President and Mrs. Reagan.

Q. Who first created aloha shirts?

A. The missionaries made them for Hawaiians to cover their torsos.

Q. How did aloha shirts develop their colorful patterns?

A. The native Hawaiians found the missionaries' shirts dull and began to paint and print designs on the shirts.

Q. What flight lost part of its fuselage in the air between the Big Island and Maui and still managed to fly to a safe landing?

A. Aloha Airlines flight 243 in April 1988.

Q. What major purchases did Japan's bachelor billionaire Gensiro Kawamoto make in Honolulu during the month of October 1987?

A. 170 houses and apartments.

Q. How many adults in Hawaii are functional illiterates with no more than the equivalent of a fifth-grade education?

A. One in every five.

Q. What is Hawaii's—and the world's—first all-Hawaiian music radio station?

A. KCCN, broadcasting since 1967.

Q. What is the pidgin word for "a large Hawaiian man"?

A. *Blalah.*

Q. What does pidgin's *like beef?* mean in English?

A. "Wanna fight?"

Q. Why do all county and state campgrounds close each Wednesday and Thursday?

A. For maintenance and to prevent permanent campsites.

Q. How did the POG craze of the 1990s originate?

A. As an Oahu schoolyard game played in the early 1970s.

Q. What were the original POGs?

A. Disposable caps on returnable glass milk bottles.

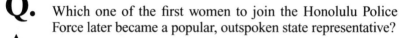

Q. How did the caps get the name *POGs*?

A. Maui's Haleakala Dairy began printing up colorful caps in 1989 to promote its mixed-juice drink called POG (passion-orange-guava).

Q. When were women allowed to join the Honoluou Police Force?

A. 1975.

Q. Which one of the first women to join the Honolulu Police Force later became a popular, outspoken state representative?

A. Annelle Amaral.

Q. On an average day, how many tourists can be found in the Islands?

A. About 160,000.

Q. What does *malihini* mean?

A. Visitor, newcomer.

Q. What does *kamaaina* mean?

A. Native-born or long-time Hawaii resident.

Q. On an average day, how many people go to the beach?

A. 170,000.

Q. In the early 1980s, what percent of tourists to Hawaii visited Oahu?

A. More than 80 percent.

Q. In the early 1990s, what percent of tourists to Hawaii visited Oahu?

A. Less than 70 percent.

Q. What is the estimated street value of Hawaii's marijuana crop every year?

A. More than $500 million.

Q. Where did the Reverend Abraham Akaka, *kahu* (shepherd) of historic Kawaiahao Church from 1957 to 1984, earn his divinity degree?

A. University of Chicago.

Q. What's the recipe for a mai tai?

A. 1¹/₂ oz. golden rum; 1¹/₂ oz. dark rum; 1 dash of rock candy syrup; 1 dash of orange syrup; 1 dash of curaçao; 1 teaspoon of lime juice; mix and serve on the rocks.

Q. What does *aloha* mean?

A. "Hello," "goodbye," or "love."

Q. How were sixty-five people living in Wainiha listed in the official 1850 government census?

A. As menehune.

Q. What is "finished, no more" in Hawaiian?

A. *Pau.*

SPORTS & RECREATION

C H A P T E R F I V E

Q. Who was the record-setting tight end from Hawaii who played for both the New England Patriots and San Francisco 49ers?

A. Russ Francis.

Q. When was surfing introduced to Hawaii?

A. Around 800 A.D. by Polynesians who migrated from the South Seas.

Q. What teams played in Hawaii's first football game in 1909?

A. The College of Hawaii and McKinley High School. The College of Hawaii won the game, six to five.

Q. What sporting event is held in the NBC Arena every April?

A. The Aloha Basketball Classic. The event is a tournament in which the nation's top basketball players are divided into four teams.

Q. Who was the first Hawaii surfer to capture the World Championship Tour title?

A. Derek Ho in 1993.

Q. What is the winner's purse in the Hawaiian Open golf tournament?

A. $216,000.

Q. Who was the first Hawaiian to win the Hawaiian Open—or any PGA tournament?

A. Ted Makalena in 1966, the year after the Hawaiian Open was founded.

Q. What happened to Ted Makalena two years after he won the Hawaiian Open?

A. He was killed in a swimming accident off Waikiki.

Q. What is ranked as one of the top kite-flying parks in the United States?

A. Kapiolani Park.

Q. What was the most popular attraction when Kapiolani Park opened in 1877?

A. Horse racing.

Q. Where is the surfing world's infamous Banzai Pipeline located?

A. At Ehukai Beach. The Pipeline is created in the curl of the twenty- to thirty-foot waves during the winter months.

Q. Who was the first person from Hawaii to compete in the Indianapolis 500?

A. Danny Ongais from Maui.

Q. Which Oahu beach is considered one of the best windsurfing sites in Hawaii?

A. Diamond Head Beach.

Q. When was the Hula Bowl first played?

A. 1947.

◆

Q. What was the official name given to the Hula Bowl in 1951?

A. The Elks Milk Fund Hula Bowl.

◆

Q. What was added to the Hawaii team in 1951 to better equip them against the more powerful Mainland opponents?

A. Players from the National Football League.

◆

Q. What is Hawaii's most popular nude beach?

A. Little Beach in Makena on the island of Maui.

◆

Q. Is nude sunbathing legal in Hawaii?

A. No. Nudists can be arrested under the state's Open Lewdness Statute.

◆

Q. Who defeated previous gold medalist swimmer Duke Kahanamoku at the Paris Olympics?

A. Johnny Weissmuller.

◆

Q. What two bowl games are held each year in Honolulu at Aloha Stadium?

A. The Pro Bowl, played by the NFL's top players, is held a week after the Super Bowl, and the Hula Bowl, featuring All-American college players, is played in mid-January.

◆

Q. How many college athletes, representing 120 college and universities, have played in the Hula Bowl since it was founded?

A. More than two thousand all-stars.

Q. Who are some of the Hula Bowl alumni?

A. William "Refrigerator" Perry, Dan Marino, Joe Montana, Troy Aikman, Dick Butkus, Fran Tarkenton, Gale Sayers, Mike Ditka, Alex Karras, Larry Csonka, Merlin Olsen, Tony Dorsett, Marcus Allen, and Ahmad Rashad.

Q. Where was Notre Dame's Heisman Trophy winner Paul Hornung rumored to finally have been found before the 1957 Hula Bowl?

A. Passed out on Waikiki Beach with a hangover.

Q. What baseball legend has a tree planted in his honor along Banyan Drive on the Big Island?

A. Babe Ruth.

Q. When did the Hula Bowl switch back to a college-players-only format?

A. 1960.

Q. When did the Hula Bowl post its first sellout?

A. In 1969 when Heisman hero Orenthal James (O.J.) Simpson played.

Q. Who holds the Hula Bowl record for the longest kickoff return (eighty-eight yards) for a touchdown?

A. O.J. Simpson in 1969.

Q. Which three current NFL players have played in all three of Hawaii's bowl games (Aloha, Hula, and Pro)?

A. Troy Aikman (with the UCLA Bruins and the Dallas Cowboys), Tim Brown (with the Fighting Irish of Notre Dame and the Oakland Raiders), and Jeff Jaeger (with the University of Hawaii Rainbows and the Oakland Raiders).

Q. When did the 1971 Hula Bowl's opposing quarterbacks, Stanford's Jim Plunkett and Notre Dame's Joe Theisman, meet again?

A. In Super Bowl XVIII—Plunkett with the Los Angeles Raiders and Theisman with the Washington Redskins.

Q. Who was the first person to ever pitch twenty winning games in the history of college baseball?

A. Derek Tatsuno, left-handed pitcher for the University of Hawaii Rainbows.

Q. What beach has given the town of Paia the distinction of windsurfing capital of the world?

A. Hookipa Beach.

Q. What is the only University of Hawaii team to win a championship in any intercollegiate sport?

A. The Rainbow Wahines volleyball team. The team won the national title in 1982 and again in 1983.

Q. Who were the first guests of millionaire Paul Fagan at his Hana Ranch Hotel, which opened in 1946?

A. Members of the San Francisco Seals baseball team, which Fagan also owned.

Q. Who was the power hitter that was part of the vacationing team?

A. Joe DiMaggio.

Q. Who was the first foreigner promoted to sumo wrestling's top rank of yokozuna in Japan?

A. Hawaii-born Chad Rowan, known as Akebono.

Q. How much does Akebono weigh?

A. More than 460 pounds.

Q. Who is the undisputed world champion of kick boxing?

A. Waikiki resident Dennis Alexio.

Q. Why was Eddie Aikau, Hawaii's champion surfer, immortalized with the popular local saying "Eddie would go"?

A. He attempted to swim fifteen miles to shore for help when he and his friends capsized aboard the *Hokulea* in 1978.

Q. Did Eddie Aikau make it to shore?

A. No, he was lost at sea.

Q. What is held in Eddie Aikau's honor every December?

A. The Eddie Aikau Big Wave Waimea Surf Classic.

Q. What is unique about the Volcano Golf and Country Club?

A. It is the only golf course in the world built along the rim of an active volcano.

Q. Who is not charged standard admission price at the Hawaii Volcanoes National Park?

A. Hawaiians who come with offerings or to perform religious rituals to Pele.

Q. Who designed Lanai's two award-winning golf courses?

A. Jack Nicklaus designed the Challenge of Manele, and Ted Robinson and Greg Norman designed the Experience at Koele.

Q. When was the Hawaii Visitors Bureau formed?

A. The Hawaii Tourist Bureau was formed in 1921 with an annual advertising budget of $125,000. By 1945 it had evolved into the Hawaii Visitors Bureau—the oldest agency of its kind in the world.

Q. In 1995, what restaurant chain became official sponsor of the Hula Bowl?

A. Hooters of America, renaming it the Hooters Hula Bowl All-Star Football Classic.

◆

Q. What does a forty-five-thousand-dollar sponsor package include at the Hertz/United Airlines Hawaiian Open Pro-Am?

A. Three Pro-Am player spots, six first-class round-trip tickets on United Airlines flights from the Mainland to Hawaii, two hundred one-day gallery viewing passes, and a corporate box on the seventeenth or eighteenth green.

◆

Q. What is Hawaii's oldest country club?

A. The Oahu Country Club. The club was built in 1906 on 373 acres once owned by Kamehameha III.

◆

Q. In what year did the Oahu Country Club finally accept Asians for membership?

A. 1968.

◆

Q. What is the course for Kona's Ironman Triathlon, founded in 1979 by John Collins?

A. A 2.4-mile rough-water open-ocean swim, a 112-mile bicycle ride, and a 26-mile marathon.

◆

Q. How much time is alloted to complete the Ironman Triathlon?

A. Seventeen hours.

◆

Q. Who was the original owner of Club 53 in Kailua-Kona?

A. Dodger pitching legend Don Drysdale.

◆

Q. Who designed the Mauna Kea Golf Course, considered the toughest course in the Islands?

A. Robert Trent Jones Sr.

Q. What is considered one of the most challenging golf course holes in the world?

A. The sixteenth hole of the Hapuna Prince Hotel golf course designed by Arnold Palmer.

Q. How high is the tee for the sixteenth hole?

A. Seven hundred feet above sea level.

SCIENCE & NATURE

C H A P T E R   S I X

Q. Considered one of the newest land masses on earth, when did the Hawaiian Islands begin forming with an underwater fissure along the Pacific Plate?

A. 70 million years ago.

Q. When did Hawaii begin to appear above the surface of the ocean?

A. 20 million years ago, when lava had eventually built high enough.

Q. How many islands, reefs, and shoals make up the Hawaiian archipelago?

A. 132, from Kure Atoll in the northwest to the Big Island of Hawaii in the southeast.

Q. How far does the Hawaiian archipelago stretch?

A. 1,523 miles.

Q. What is the total land area of the Hawaiian Islands?

A. 6,470 square miles.

Q. What percent of United States land is made up by the state of Hawaii?

A. 0.2 percent.

———◆———

Q. What states are smaller than Hawaii?

A. Connecticut, Delaware, and Rhode Island.

———◆———

Q. What state has more shark attacks than Hawaii?

A. Florida, with an average of thirteen per year.

———◆———

Q. What are the latitudes and longititudes of the Hawaiian Islands?

A. Between latitudes 28° 15' and 18° 54'N and longititudes 179° 25' and 154° 40'W, making it the southernmost state in the United States.

———◆———

Q. Hawaii is the only state where the sun does what twice a year?

A. Stands directly overhead at noon—once in May and again in July.

———◆———

Q. Snow falls every winter on what two volcanic peaks in Hawaii?

A. The Big Island's Mauna Kea and Mauna Loa.

———◆———

Q. What type of whales migrate through Hawaiian waters every November through June, with the best observation points occurring near Lahaina?

A. Humpback whales.

———◆———

Q. How big can humpbacks grow?

A. As long as forty-five feet and weighing up to forty tons.

Q. Why are scrimshaw pieces now engraved on fossilized walrus tusks and not whale teeth?

A. Whale teeth are protected by the Endangered Species Act of 1973.

◆

Q. The steady trade winds blowing out of the northeast give Honolulu what distinction?

A. The seventh windiest city in America.

◆

Q. Hawaii is the only state subject to what four natural disasters?

A. Volcanic eruptions, earthquakes, hurricanes, and tsunamis.

◆

Q. How many shark attacks occur in Hawaii every year?

A. An average of four.

◆

Q. What is the only national, privately supported botanical garden chartered by Congress?

A. The National Tropical Botanical Garden, chartered in 1964.

◆

Q. The 186-acre National Tropical Botanical Garden includes what estate?

A. The Allerton Estate. This estate was the former vacation home of Queen Emma, wife of Kamehameha IV.

◆

Q. The giant green lily pads in the ponds of the National Tropical Botanical Garden are capable of supporting the weight of what?

A. A standing, medium-sized man.

◆

Q. What is the southernmost spot in the United States?

A. Ka Lae, south point on the Big Island of Hawaii.

Q. What islands in the Hawaiian chain are administered by the U.S. Navy?

A. The Midway Islands.

Q. What six of the eight main islands in the Hawaiian chain may tourists visit?

A. Kauai, Lanai, Maui, Molokai, Oahu, and the Big Island. Niihau is privately owned, and Kahoolawe is not inhabited.

Q. Which Hawaiian island was once used by the military for target practice?

A. Kahoolawe.

Q. What land masses are nearest to Hawaii?

A. California is 2,390 miles to the east-northeast, the Marquesas are 2,400 miles to the south-southeast, Japan is 3,850 miles to the west-northwest, and Alaska is 2,600 miles to the north.

Q. What are the two Hawaiian names geologists commonly use for lava?

A. *Pahoehoe* (a fluid lava flow that dries to a smooth surface) and *Aa* (a slow moving flow that dries with a rough and jagged crust).

Q. What is *vog*?

A. A fog caused by sulfuric volcanic fumes mixing with oxygen.

Q. What is *laze*?

A. A haze from steam created by molten lava flowing into the ocean.

Q. How many native plants and birds are found in the Hawaiian Islands?

A. More than 3,000.

Q. How many Hawaiian plants and birds are on the endangered list?

A. 710.

Q. How many Hawaiian plants and birds are now listed as extinct?

A. 251.

Q. How many native fish are found in Hawaiian waters?

A. More than 200.

Q. What was declared the official flower of Hawaii in 1923?

A. The hibiscus.

Q. How long does a hibiscus flower last once it blooms?

A. Only a few hours before withering.

Q. What is unique about the feet of the nene goose, the state bird?

A. The nene's feet are claw-like rather than webbed, adapted for its life in lava fields.

Q. What other bird is a relative of the nene?

A. The Canadian goose.

Q. What almost drove the nene to extinction?

A. Predators such as rats and mongooses.

Q. What does the name of the state fish, *Humuhu-munukunukuapuaa*, mean in Hawaiian?

A. The name of the small common fish with a long uncommon name means "to fit pieces together with a nose like a pig."

Q. Visiting Hawaiian waters every year during its annual migration, what distinction did the humpback whale receive in 1979?

A. It was named the official state marine mammal of Hawaii.

Q. What plant is only found on the higher zones of the Big Island and Maui?

A. The silversword, which only grows in volcanic rock at levels of six thousand feet or more.

Q. How many times does a silversword bloom?

A. After taking more than twenty years to mature, the silversword will bloom only once with flower stalks as high as eight feet and covered with as many as five hundred individual blossoms. It then dies.

Q. What flower only blooms at night?

A. The night-blooming cereus. The large blossoms of the Mexican cactus open around nine in the evening and close before sunrise.

Q. Why was the mongoose imported to Hawaii in the 1880s?

A. To eradicate rodents that were destroying Island crops.

Q. What was wrong with this plan?

A. The rat is nocturnal; the mongoose is not.

Q. What did the mongoose eradicate?

A. The mongoose was responsible for the extinction of many native ground-nesting birds.

Q. Hawaii's production of macadamia nuts makes up what percent of the world's supply?

A. More than 90 percent.

Q. When were macadamia nut trees introduced to Hawaii from Australia?

A. In the mid-1880s as ornamental trees.

Q. When was the first macadamia nut plantation started on the Big Island?

A. 1921.

Q. How long did it take the University of Hawaii to develop the macadamia nut sold in markets today?

A. Twenty years.

Q. What type of tree is the macadamia?

A. A subtropical evergreen.

Q. How old is a macadamia when it first bears nuts?

A. Five years.

Q. When does a macadamia reach its productivity peak?

A. When it has matured to its fifteenth year.

Q. When was the pineapple introduced to Hawaii?

A. Sometime between 1778 and 1813 by Spanish traders.

Q. What native birds, thought to be extinct, have been discovered nesting on Maui?

A. The nukupuu and akohekoha, a family of birds that developed uniquely curved bills to sip nectar from island flowers.

◆

Q. What new species of Hawaiian bird was discovered on the northeast slope of Haleakala in 1973?

A. The honeycreeper poouli.

◆

Q. What sea animal was a popular food with Hawaii's monarchy?

A. The Hawaiian green sea turtle.

◆

Q. How did the endangered Hawaiian green sea turtle get its name?

A. From the color of its body fat.

◆

Q. Where have more than half of Hawaii's recent shark attacks occured in the past few years?

A. Off Oahu beaches.

◆

Q. How many people have been killed from shark attacks since 1960?

A. Two, a female swimmer in 1991 off Maui and a surfer in 1992 off Oahu's north shore.

◆

Q. What happened every one thousand years, on average, during the formation of the Islands?

A. A new life-form found its way to the Islands.

◆

Q. What has happened to the most northwest islands that were part of the Hawaiian Island chain?

A. They have eroded to become underwater seamounts.

Q. How many cubic miles in bulk is Mauna Loa?

A. Ten thousand cubic miles. It is one hundred times larger than Mount Shasta or Mount Fuji.

Q. How many years did it take Mauna Loa to rise from sea level to its current height of 13,796 feet?

A. Fewer than five hundred thousand years.

Q. What is studied in Science City at Haleakala's summit?

A. The sun.

Q. What must astronomers atop the Big Island's Mauna Kea remember to do every four days?

A. They must come down to sea level. The thin air can make them forgetful.

Q. What is the Mauna Kea Shadow?

A. A phenomenon that occurs at sunset when the volcano casts its own shadow against clouds in the sky.

Q. What two universities jointly operate a gamma ray telescope on Haleakala?

A. Purdue University and the University of Wisconsin.

Q. What is the nickname of the national defense project experiments in which the U.S. Air Force beams lasers from Haleakala to orbiting satellites and back?

A. Star Wars.

Q. What were the first two mammals to settle in the Islands?

A. A hoary bat settled on land, and a monk seal, at sea.

Q. How many Hawaiian monk seals still exist?

A. Fewer than fifteen hundred, which explains why the mammal is on the endangered species list.

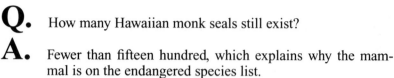

Q. How many species of native Hawaiian insects have been found in the Islands?

A. More than ten thousand.

Q. How many species of land snails have been found in Hawaii?

A. More than one thousand.

Q. How many types of flowering plants bloom in the Islands?

A. Approximately eighteen hundred.

Q. Why are Hawaiian tussock grasslands unique?

A. They are the only tropical subalpine grasslands on earth.

Q. What animal can only be found near Puu Wekiu, the snow-covered summit of Mauna Kea?

A. The wingless wekiu bug.

Q. What has the wekiu bug developed?

A. Antifreeze blood.

Q. What happens when one holds the wekiu bug in one's hand?

A. The heat of the hand cooks the bug's proteins.

Q. What type of fumes are released by the volcanoes?

A. Sulfurous fumes.

Q. What is the area called that remains green in the midst of a lava flow?

A. A kipuka.

Q. How long does it take for a forest of ohia lehua trees to develop on a lava flow?

A. Fewer than one hundred years.

Q. What is unique about the subterranean lava tube cricket?

A. It has no eyes or wings.

Q. What happened in 1923 to the last three Laysan honey-creepers on earth?

A. While a scientific expedition watched, they were killed in a sudden sandstorm on an atoll in the Hawaiian Islands—the first and only time mankind has witnessed the extinction of a songbird.

Q. Which is the only island where you can still spot an io (Hawaiian hawk)?

A. The Big Island.

Q. Where are the world's only two forests of native Hawaiian loulu palms?

A. Atop the 220-foot Huelo Island spire off the coast of Molokai and on the remote Nihoa Island north of Kauai.

Q. What does the ihiihilauakea fern, which only grows on the island of Oahu, resemble?

A. A four-leaf clover.

Q. What name did scientists give to trees discovered growing in a small forest on Molokai in 1980?

A. Lobelia.

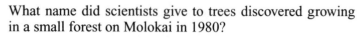

Q. Why did ancient Hawaiians dedicate the ieie vine to Ku, ruler of all male gods and humankind?

A. They believed the orange blossom of the vine was a spiritual link between the islands and the heavens.

Q. How many species of violets are found in Hawaii?

A. Seven.

Q. How tall do Hawaiian violet flower stems grow?

A. More than two feet high.

Q. How long do Hawaiian dryland trees hold their leaves each year?

A. Only two months, usually after winter rains.

Q. What is the most widespread plant of the Hawaiian Islands?

A. The ohia.

Q. What type of grass prevents the seeds of native trees from germinating by absorbing moisture around the roots?

A. Kikuyu, a grass brought to the islands from Africa.

Q. What is unique about the pueo (Hawaiian owl)?

A. It flies by day.

Q. What does the pueo hunt by day?

A. Rats, mice, and small birds.

Q. What is a relative of mao (Hawaiian cotton)?

A. Hibiscus.

Q. The iliahi, most fragrant of the nearly extinct Hawaiian sandalwood trees, grows only on what island?

A. The slopes of eastern Maui.

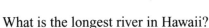

Q. What do Hawaiian dry forests have more of than Hawaiian rain forests?

A. Varieties of trees.

Q. What is the longest river in Hawaii?

A. Wailuku River. It is eighteen miles long and flows near Hilo on the Big Island.

Q. What two species of birds are found only in Molokai's Kamakou Preserve?

A. The Molokai thrush and the Molokai creeper.

Q. How does the aukuu, an Island bird, catch fish or shrimp?

A. By spearing it with its narrow, sharp beak.

Q. Why are there so few lakes in Hawaii?

A. Volcanic soil is too permeable.

Q. What is distinctive about Lake Waiau near the summit of Mauna Kea?

A. It is the highest lake in Hawaii.

Q. What is the estimated feral pig population in Hawaiian rain forests?

A. Greater than fifty thousand.

Q. What damage is caused by the passion fruit vine, introduced to Hawaii from South America?

A. The vine grows to engulf trees and eventually suffocates them.

Q. What Kauai bird, common at the turn of the century, is now thought to be extinct?

A. The oo.

Q. How many native butterfly species are found in Hawaii?

A. Two, including the Kamehameha or pulelehua butterfly.

Q. What is the name of Hawaii's only carnivorous plant?

A. The mikinalo, or "fly-sucker."

Q. What is unique about the Hawaiian caterpillar?

A. It is the only known predatory caterpillar in the world, feeding on insects.

Q. What do Hawaiian tree snails do as they crawl across leaves?

A. Clean the plants of harmful algae and molds.

Q. How close is the nearest tropical rain forest to the snow-covered summit of Mauna Kea?

A. Five miles.

———◆———

Q. What is Hawaii's most abundant bird?

A. The Japanese white-eye.

———◆———

Q. In what year was the Japanese white-eye brought to Oahu from the Orient?

A. 1929.

———◆———

Q. What is Hawaii's most abundant native bird?

A. The apapane, found only in elevations above three thousand feet.

———◆———

Q. What is the name of the yellow-white-and-gray bird that lays blue eggs?

A. The red-billed leothrix. It was brought to Hawaii from China in 1911.

———◆———

Q. During what year was the bright red northern cardinal introduced to the islands from North America?

A. 1929.

———◆———

Q. Why were mynah birds brought to Hawaii from India in 1865?

A. To control insects in sugar cane fields.

———◆———

Q. What did the zebra dove carry when it was brought to the Islands in 1922?

A. Diseases that killed many of Hawaii's native birds.

Q. Why were gray falcolins brought to Molokai from India in 1958?

A. To be hunted as game birds.

Q. What is Hawaii's most common seabird?

A. Wedge-tailed shearwaters.

Q. When were the destructive axis deer introduced to Hawaii?

A. 1868 as a gift to King Kamehameha V.

Q. What color are bougainvillea flowers?

A. White. Pigmented leaves around the tiny white flowers give the vine its bright colors.

Q. Where are Hawaii's only four known patches of the endangered false jade plant growing?

A. Two on islets off of Molokai, one on Wailea, and one at Maui's Kahului Zoo.

Q. What does the name of the fruit-bearing vine "passion fruit" refer to?

A. The sufferings of Christ. Each portion of the vine symbolizes one aspect of the Crucifixion.

Q. What do the flowers of Turk's cap resemble?

A. Unopened hibiscus blossoms.

Q. What are the three principal reef-building corals in Hawaii?

A. Montipora, pocillopora, and porites species.

Q. What is Penguin Bank off Molokai?

A. A forty-mile underwater shelf.

———◆———

Q. What did Penguin Bank used to be?

A. An island. It eventually eroded beneath the sea about seventeen thousand years ago.

———◆———

Q. When were Madagascar's bright red royal poinciana trees brought to Hawaii?

A. 1855.

———◆———

Q. What are sweet onions grown on Molokai known as in markets across the world?

A. Maui onions.

———◆———

Q. How many plumeria blossoms does it take to make a standard lei?

A. Fifty.

———◆———

Q. What is Hawaii's highest seacliff?

A. Molokai's Olokui Plateau with cliffs thirty-five hundred feet above the sea.

———◆———

Q. How long does a piece of sandalwood hold its fragrance?

A. About fifty years.

———◆———

Q. How did traders discover Hawaiian forests were full of sandalwood trees?

A. A ship's captain cooked dinner in 1790 over sandalwood firewood purchased on Kauai.

Q. What was Hawaiian sandalwood used for?

A. Incense, body oils, perfumes, and household and religious ornaments.

◆

Q. Why were Hawaiian forests stripped of sandalwood?

A. Hawaiian chiefs needed to pay off more than $4 million in debt for luxuries such as tobacco and alcohol bought from traders.

◆

Q. What is happening off the southeastern shore of the Big Island?

A. A new island named Loihi is forming.

◆

Q. How far below the surface is the new island?

A. One-half mile.

◆

Q. In what year was the first written account of Kilauea's eruptions recorded?

A. 1823, by missionary William Ellis.

◆

Q. Who was the first resident geologist at Kilauea in 1909?

A. Thomas A. Jagger. He was formerly a geology professor at the Massachusetts Institute of Technology.

◆

Q. When Jagger lowered the first thermometer into Halemaumau's lava lake in 1911, what did it register before it melted?

A. 1,832° F.

◆

Q. Who proposed a bill to Congress in 1911 and again in 1915 to create Kilauea National Park?

A. Hawaii congressional delegate Prince Jonah Kuhio Kalanianaole.

Q. In what year did Jagger found the Hawaiian Volcano Observatory?

A. 1912.

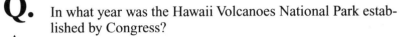

Q. In what year was the Hawaii Volcanoes National Park established by Congress?

A. 1916.

Q. What is unique about Hawaii's volcano eruptions?

A. Eruptions occur not only at volcano summits but also from side rift zones.

Q. How many square miles make up the Hawaii Volcanoes National Park?

A. 377 square miles—more than the entire island of Molokai.

———◆———

Q. What is "Pele's Curse"?

A. The bad luck that will plague anyone who removes lava rocks from the Hawaii Volcanoes National Park.

———◆———

Q. Who created "Pele's Curse"?

A. A park ranger in 1946, to discourage visitors from taking lava rocks as souvenirs of the area.

———◆———

Q. How many pounds of lava rock are mailed back each year to park headquarters, many with letters detailing their bad luck and offering apologies to Pele?

A. More than two thousand pounds.

———◆———

Q. When did the Coast Guard stop manning Kilauea Lighthouse, built in 1913, and install an automated light?

A. 1967.

Q. What organization now operates the Kilauea Lighthouse?

A. The U.S. Fish and Wildlife Service, which concentrates on the thirty-one-acre bird sanctuary surrounding the lighthouse.

MYTHS & LEGENDS

C H A P T E R   S E V E N

Q. What two plants do Hawaiians plant around their homes for good luck?

A. Ti and bird of paradise.

———◆———

Q. Of the more than forty thousand Hawaiian gods, who are the four greatest?

A. Kane, Kanaloa, Ku, and Lono.

———◆———

Q. Who was Maui?

A. A Hawaiian demigod with Herculean strength.

———◆———

Q. What was Maui's greatest feat?

A. While on a fishing expedition in the Pacific, he hooked the Hawaiian Islands and raised them to the surface.

———◆———

Q. According to Hawaiian legend, what still lives in the mountain pools above Hanalei on Kauai?

A. The moo, a giant lizard god.

Q. What did Ku rule over?

A. All male gods and all humankind.

Q. Who ruled over female gods?

A. Ku's wife, Hina.

Q. What did Kanaloa rule?

A. The dead.

Q. What did Lono rule?

A. The stars, the moon, and all the elements of earth.

Q. What did Kane create?

A. Man, made from the dust of the Islands.

Q. How high is the spire of Iao Needle?

A. Twelve hundred feet.

Q. Who was Iao?

A. Maui's daughter.

Q. What is Iao Needle?

A. Iao's unfaithful lover, whom Maui turned to stone.

Q. Who were the menehune?

A. Hawaii's mythical race of industrious little people.

———◆———

Q. What is an explanation for the menehune's existence?

A. They were short Marquesans, forced to do labor for the conquering Tahitians migrating to the islands around 1000 A.D.

———◆———

Q. Who lives in the caves beneath Rainbow Falls on the Big Island?

A. The goddess Hina, mother of Maui.

———◆———

Q. Why is the large rock in Wailuku River called Maui's Canoe?

A. According to the myth, the demigod Maui paddled his canoe so fast across the sea that he crashed here and his canoe turned to stone.

———◆———

Q. Why did Hawaiians name Maui's volcano Haleakala (House of the Sun)?

A. According to the legend, Maui, at the request of his mother Hina, lassoed the hurried sun from the summit of the volcano. Tying it to a wiliwili tree, he made the sun promise to move more slowly across Hawaiian skies before releasing it.

———◆———

Q. Ancient Hawaiians believed Molokai was the daughter of what goddess?

A. Hina, goddess of the moon and mother of Maui.

———◆———

Q. Who is Pele?

A. Goddess of fire and the volcanoes.

———◆———

Q. What was Pele's full name?

A. Peleai Honua, (the Earth Eater).

Q. What power was believed to be found in the chair-shaped Hauola Stone, located at the base of the seawall in Lahaina Harbor?

A. The power to restore good health by sitting on the stone and letting the waves wash over you.

Q. Who were Pele's mother and father?

A. Her mother was Haumea, goddess of fertility; her father was Wakea, ruler of the sky.

Q. How did Pele travel?

A. As a fireball.

Q. Who was Hawaii's original fire god who fled the islands when Pele arrived from her native Kahiki?

A. Ailaau.

Q. Who chased Pele across the seas and islands of Hawaii?

A. Her sister, Namaka, goddess of the sea, who never forgave Pele for ravaging the land.

Q. Why did Pele leave Haleakala?

A. The volcano was too large to keep her warm.

Q. Where did Namaka finally destroy Pele?

A. Near Hana, where Namaka tore Pele's body apart and scattered her bones at Kahikinui.

Q. Where did Pele's spirit finally settle?

A. In the Halemaumau fire pit of Kilauea on the Big Island.

Q. How does Pele regularly get revenge on Namaka?

A. By sending flows of molten lava into the ocean, boiling the seas of Namaka.

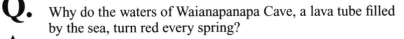

Q. Why do the waters of Waianapanapa Cave, a lava tube filled by the sea, turn red every spring?

A. According to the legend, it is the blood of a Hawaiian princess, mistakenly killed by her jealous husband in the month of April as she hid from him in the cave. Another reason may be the high density of red opaeula shrimp.

Q. According to a Hawaiian creation chant, where did Kane create the very first man?

A. On Mokapu peninsula, current site of the Marine Corps Air Station, on the windward side of Oahu.

Q. Who is Poliahu?

A. Snow goddess of Mauna Kea.

Q. Who made his home atop the 260-foot cinderhill Kauiki Head?

A. The demigod Maui.

Q. Who brought the hula, the traditional Hawaiian dance, to the islands?

A. Two gods from Tahiti, one male and one female, who were both named Laka.

Q. The female Laka was both sister and wife of what god?

A. Lono, one of the four major gods of Hawaii.

Q. What was the significance of Kauleonanahoan (phallic rock) located inside Palaau State Park?

A. Childless women who spent the night at the base of the six-foot rock would soon become pregnant.

Q. What does *Kauleonanahoa* mean?

A. Nanahoa's penis.

Q. Who taught the hula to the people of Hawaii?

A. The female Laka, who was left to dance by herself when the male Laka returned to Tahiti.

Q. Who was one of the first to learn the dance?

A. Hiiaka, the youngest sister of Pele.

Q. Why were Hawaiians frightened of Lanai?

A. They believed the island to be inhabited by evil spirits.

Q. When did Hawaiians begin to settle on Lanai?

A. Not until Kaululaau, the law-breaking son of a Maui chief who was exiled to the island, supposedly killed off the demons.

Q. What explanation is offered for the mysterious sound sometimes heard inside Iolani Palace?

A. According to popular belief, the sound is that of keys being rattled by King Kalakaau's gatekeeper.

Q. What is "the Sadness Spirit"?

A. An unexplained glow of light that sometimes appears through the window of the second floor room of Iolani Palace where Queen Liliuokalani was imprisoned following her overthrow.

Q. What two ghosts reportedly haunt the state capitol?

A. Queen Liliuokalani, walking barefoot through the halls, and the late Gov. John A. Burns.

Q. What ghost haunts the area between the state capitol and Iolani Palace?

A. A Hawaiian woman in a long white muumuu described as a "calling spirit" who calls out to passers-by.

◆

Q. What used to stand on the site of the Territorial Building, where cries of babies are sometimes mysteriously heard?

A. The Oahu Charity School.

◆

Q. According to legend, who dug Kauhako Crater on Molokai?

A. Pele, Hawaii's fire goddess.

◆

Q. Why did Pele leave Molokai?

A. She struck water in Kauhako Crater and moved on to Maui.

◆

Q. What ghost has been spotted at the Kahala Mall?

A. A faceless, legless woman—the same that used to haunt the women's restroom at the old Waialae Drive-In across the street.

◆

Q. Where was the original and most sacred school of hula, the traditional Hawaiian dance?

A. On the slopes of Mauna Loa, which is the site every May of the Molokai Ka Hula Piko festival.

◆

Q. Who is believed to be the founder of the hula school?

A. Kapo, a sister of fire goddess Pele.

◆

Q. What is Hula Halau Heiau in Haena State Park?

A. The temple where Pele was believed to have danced and where women would come to learn the art of the hula, the traditional Hawaiian dance.

Q. Who is the goddess of hula, still honored with offerings at Hula Halau Heiau?

A. Laka.

Q. Why did ancient Hawaiian women place their babies' umbilical cords (*piko*) around the Maunaloa Piko stone?

A. To guarantee a prosperous life for their newborns.

Q. Homeless Hawaiian ghosts are often spotted at what Honolulu intersection?

A. The corner of Alakea and Queen streets.

Q. What father of a United States senator exorcised those possessed by the dreaded Japanese demon dog spirits?

A. Kingoro Matsunaga, father of U.S. Sen. Spark Matsunaga of Hawaii.

Q. What are *akua lele*?

A. Fireballs, which some Hawaiians believe to be flying spirits of the dead.

Q. Where are akua lele frequently seen?

A. At Makapuu Point, Sacred Falls, and over Iolani Palace.

Q. What are the twin pillars at Alakoko fish pond?

A. According to local mythology, the pillars are a princess and her brother who were warned not to watch the menehune build the fish pond or else they would be turned to stone.

Q. If a fisherman spots two uhu (parrotfish) rubbing noses or leaping out of the water, what does that signify?

A. The fisherman's wife is being unfaithful.

Q. If the bright red aweoweo fish swim in a large cluster, what will happen?

A. Someone of importance will soon die.

Q. According to local Hawaiian superstitions, what can cause bad luck if done in a house?

A. Whistling, sweeping at night, and sleeping with one's feet pointed toward the door.

Q. What will happen if a person throws a flower lei into the ocean when leaving the islands and it floats back to shore?

A. That person will return to the islands someday.

Q. Where did a high chief sacrifice nine of the ten sons of a Molokai farmer?

A. Iliiliopae Heiau—one of the largest temples built in the islands.

Q. How big was Iliiliopae Heiau?

A. Five acres.

Q. How long did it take to build?

A. According to legend, the heaiu was built in one night by the menehune, Hawaii's mythical little people.

Q. Where did the god Lono meet Kaikilani, one of his wives?

A. In the rainbow around Hiilawe Falls.

Q. What is believed to live in the pool at the base of Moaula Falls?

A. Water spirits.

Q. How can you tell if the water spirits are in a good mood?

A. It is safe to swim in the pool only if a ti leaf thrown in the water floats. If the leaf sinks, the water spirits are looking for another victim.

◆

Q. Who were Lehua and Maile?

A. The mistresses of the Hawaiian god Akaka. Akaka fell to his death over what is now the 442-foot Akaka Falls.

◆

Q. What became of Lehua and Maile?

A. The women turned into two smaller waterfalls in a nearby ravine when they could not stop crying.

◆

Q. What can be seen from the town of Kapaa?

A. The Sleeping Giant Ridge. According to legend, it was formed when a Hawaiian giant stuffed himself at a laua and fell into an eternal nap.

◆

Q. What are the Three Sisters on Kauai?

A. Three peaks in Kalalau Valley, popularly believed to be goddesses that were turned to stone by their angry father when he caught them helping mortals.

◆

Q. Where does Pele, the goddess of fire, now reside?

A. Halemaumau, on the Big Island.

Bio

Q. Who is Ed. Cassidy?

A. A native of Hawaii and graduate of Punahou School in Honolulu. Former editor and publisher of *Honolulu Magazine*, he is now a marketing executive with Gannett's *The Tennessean* and *Nashville Banner*.

———◆———

Q. Who does Ed. Cassidy thank for their assistance with *Hawaii Trivia*?

A. Mahalo to Edith Cassidy, Elissa Josephsohn, Wayne Harada, Eddie Sherman, Janice Otaguro, Beverly Fujita, Marilyn Kim, Bonnie Landrum, Lee Davenport, Kokea Landrum, and a very special mahalo nui loa to Charles Landrum.